OUR ONLY HOPE

WILLIAM W. RICHMOND

WESTBOW
PRESS®
A DIVISION OF THOMAS NELSON
& ZONDERVAN

WestBow Press books may be ordered through booksellers or by contacting:

WestBow Press
A Division of Thomas Nelson & Zondervan
1663 Liberty Drive
Bloomington, IN 47403
www.westbowpress.com
1 (866) 928-1240

Because of the dynamic nature of the Internet, any web addresses or links contained in this book may have changed since publication and may no longer be valid. The views expressed in this work are solely those of the author and do not necessarily reflect the views of the publisher, and the publisher hereby disclaims any responsibility for them.

Scriptures taken from the Holy Bible, New International Version®, NIV®. Copyright © 1973, 1978, 1984, 2011 by Biblica, Inc.™ Used by permission of Zondervan. All rights reserved worldwide. www.zondervan.com The "NIV" and "New International Version" are trademarks registered in the United States Patent and Trademark Office by Biblica, Inc.™

Any people depicted in stock imagery provided by Thinkstock are models, and such images are being used for illustrative purposes only. Certain stock imagery © Thinkstock.

ISBN: 978-1-9736-1813-3 (sc)
ISBN: 978-1-9736-1814-0 (hc)
ISBN: 978-1-9736-0129-6 (e)

Library of Congress Control Number: 2018901368

Print information available on the last page.

WestBow Press rev. date: 01/31/2018

To you, my Lord and Savior, Jesus Christ. Without you, this project would not have been possible. I came to know you on April 1, 1997, and my life has not been the same since that day. Through all my trials, hardships, and mistakes, I could not out-sin your love. This book is just a small contribution to the amazing love you have shown me. Thank you for never forsaking me and giving me the strength, courage, and wisdom to push forward. Thank you for believing in me even when I didn't believe in myself.

FOREWORD

William Richmond has an amazing and inspirational true-life story of triumph in the face of adversity, pain, sorrow, and loss. William experienced hardships of so many kinds, including physical challenges, the loss of his sight, and the loss of a leg because of an accident. He also experienced relational heartbreak in his marriage, the struggle of addiction, and a broken home. Although William has been through incredible times of struggle and often unexpected and seemingly unfair circumstances, he carries on with his life today with amazing and perhaps even miraculous strength, determination, and joy!

Although he is no longer able to walk on the same two legs, he was born with, and even though he can no longer see, William walks, participates in sports, and carries on with almost all of life's events in ways that seem almost effortless and oftentimes unassisted. What is more important is that he is living every day of his life now with a smile on his face! William has been given new and exciting opportunities and relationships with people to love. Any person who would read his story would be staggered in seeing the peace and stability that he has attained. How did William manage to find so much purpose, hope, and strength for a life that seems to have lost so much? The answer might be surprising!

Although William wrestled with physical, emotional, mental, and relational issues, he discovered his hope, purpose, and strength for life from the spiritual things! He came face-to-face with spiritual truths and love that he could not deny or turn away from. From these things, he found the inner strength, peace, and power that gave him the greatest quality of life (which can be experienced in even the toughest times).

However, something even more valuable happened for William. Not only did he find hope and purpose for life, but William changed! It is undeniable that William is a different person now than he was years ago. He improved in so many ways as a result of submitting to the spiritual truths of the hope of salvation. What William discovered weren't just answers for his problems. He literally discovered how to have new life!

If you are dealing with hardship, pain, or loss, there is hope. If you think you have run out of chances, there really are new and fresh opportunities that await you. If you feel empty even though you see and have so much in life, you can find what is truly fulfilling. Read on with an open mind and an open heart, and hear the true story of how God transformed and brought unimaginable blessing to a man who was seemingly losing it all.

ACKNOWLEDGMENTS

Thanks to my family and friend who have supported me on this project and spent countless hours of their own time helping me see this through. This would not have been possible without you. To all of you, I give my deepest gratitude.

CHAPTER 1

Have mercy on me, O God, have mercy on me, for
in you my soul takes refuge. I will take refuge in the
shadow of your wings until the disaster has passed.

—Psalm 57:1

THE BRIGHT LIGHTS from an occasional car passing in the
opposite lane were the only things keeping me from nodding
off in the passenger seat of the Bronco. I had agreed to accompany
my friend Steve to his hometown so he could take care of some
family business. Steve, who did not own a vehicle, asked if we
could use my recently purchased Bronco with four-wheel drive,
equipped with spotlights on the roof, running boards, and big
tires for the road trip. The Bronco looked like something a Texas
Ranger would drive, and I was extremely proud of my new truck!
Steve offered to drive since he knew where we were going, and
I gladly let him.

Steve and I were great friends, and after he finished his
business, he showed me around the town. We went to a few
nightclubs and stopped at a local diner to get something to eat
before the long journey home.

As we drove along, I thought about how different my life
had been only a month before. Since birth, I had been visually

impaired. I struggled to get through school, reading the large print on the outside of the books to barely pass each class. Then I dropped out of school in the ninth grade. My sight seemed to hold steady for many years, and then I found that I was struggling to see the keypad on the telephone. What I was able to see not long ago was now getting blurry. I panicked. "Am I going blind?" I asked myself. It didn't help that I thought my sight would not improve. "What will I do for work? How will I take care of my family?" I was not one for feeling sorry for myself, but the thought of blindness was almost more than I could stand. I couldn't help but to feel a little depressed.

I didn't have any choice but to tell Shelly, my wife, that I believed I was going blind.

Afterward, she was very concerned, but unlike me, she was not willing to think the worst until I went to a doctor. That, however, was not my first choice. Since I'd been a child, the doctors had told me that I wouldn't go blind, but now my eyes were getting worse. I wasn't ready to hear more of the same from some brainiac doctor.

Eventually, I relented and went for an eye examination. Shelly insisted on seeing one of the best eye doctors in the area. I agreed, but I was sure it would not make any difference.

After hours of testing, I was getting anxious. The doctor arrived a short time later and said, "The bad news is that you have severe damage to your eyes since birth."

To be kind, I shook my head as if to say, "I know," but I was really thinking, *No kidding! Is this what I sat here all day for?*

A moment later, I got the surprise of my life. The doctor said, "The good news is that I can improve your vision."

What is this guy? I thought. *A mad scientist?*

"You have juvenile cataracts," he said.

Shelly sat with her eyes widened, and I was in disbelief! After questioning the doctor, I realized that the cataracts were the reason for the declining vision. The doctor assured me that outpatient cataract surgery would significantly improve my vision.

I scheduled the surgery, and a week later, Shelly drove me back to the eye center for the operation on my left eye. The surgery seemed simple enough, but I wanted to think that something would go wrong. *What if his hand slips?* I thought as panic began to overtake me.

However, it was a success, and the following week, the surgery on my right eye was equally successful. It seemed like in no time at all before the patches were off my eyes and I could see better than I could ever remember. I was amazed!

After going home that day, I started picking objects up just to look at them. I picked up the telephone, and it looked like the numbers were jumping out at me! Next, I looked at the newspaper and couldn't believe that I could read the fine print.

A few minutes later, when Shelly came home from work, I was still picking up things to find out what I could actually see. "What are you doing?" she asked.

"I can see! I can really see things that I couldn't see before!" Truly amazed at my sight, I exclaimed, "Do you think I could get my driver's license?"

After studying for a couple of weeks, I passed both sections of the driver's test. The officer called my name to give me my driver's license, and when he handed it to me, I just stood there and stared at it! I couldn't believe that I was finely able to drive! The officer didn't know what to make of me staring at the license and asked, "That is you, isn't it?"

"Oh yes, it's me!" I shouted as I hurried out the door to tell Shelly the good news.

Within a week, I bought the Bronco!

As I was thinking about how that day had changed everything, I noticed Steve jerking his head to look at the dashboard. He looked over at me and said, "I forgot to stop and get gas, and we are almost out! I know if we turn around, we won't make it back to town."

We pulled off to the side of the road to regroup. "What do you think we should do?" Steve asked. "We know we will not make it back to town, and it appears that we passed the road heading west that would take us home."

We were not sure how far the next gas station was, so I thought we should go for it. "Keep driving!" I said.

As Steve pulled back onto the highway, our eyes scanned the dark, desolate road for anything that resembled the illumination of a gas station sign.

A few minutes later, the Bronco's engine began to sputter, and Steve navigated the vehicle to the berm of the road. He exclaimed, "That's it! We are out of gas!"

We just sat there in silence, trying to come up with a brilliant plan that might get us out of what seemed like a very bad situation. Fortunately, I had a gas can in the back of the truck.

As I retrieved it, Steve looked up the road in front of us and said, "There is a gas station up there somewhere, but I'm not sure how far." He extended his hand for me to give him the gas can.

I said, "No, you stay here with the truck. I'll go."

That fateful decision would change my life and the lives of my family forever.

It would have made more sense for Steve to go. He could see better, and he knew the area. However, it was almost as if I felt a need to go, and I just couldn't say no. I had to be the one to go for gas, and I had to do it on my own.

I took the gas can and started kicking stones as I walked up the side of the road. Before I was too far away, Steve yelled, "Are you sure you don't want me to go?"

"No, I'll be okay!" I shouted.

I couldn't have been more wrong.

It's kind of spooky out here! I thought as I heard something stirring in the weeds a few yards to my right. I remembered that many different kinds of wild animals, such as alligators and wild boar, lived in this part of the state. As I heard a lone car approaching, I turned around and attempted to hitchhike. It was then that I noticed the silhouette of the Bronco disappearing. The car zoomed by with no intention of stopping. Traffic was sparse on this part of the highway, especially at midnight. I continued my journey in the oppressive darkness for a while longer without another single car passing by. The night was quiet, except for the rustling of some creatures in the weeds.

Fear quickly turned into a strange, euphoric feeling that moved from the top of my head to the tips of my toes. It was an amazing feeling that I had never felt before. It startled me, not in a frightening sort of way but to the point that I stopped to look around. I'm not sure what I thought I might find, but nothing looked out of the ordinary. I thought, *I know what it feels like to be intoxicated, and this is not the same. It's like a sense of peace and comfort all wrapped into one.* As I was contemplating what this all meant, the sound of an approaching car engine brought me back to the reason why I was walking on this dark, desolate road. This car sped right by just like the first one.

In what seemed like just seconds later, another car started approaching, but this one sounded like it was traveling much faster than the last two. As I spun around to stick out my thumb, I was met by blinding headlights. It happened so fast that I didn't have a chance to get out of the way as the car tossed me in the air like a rag doll; I began to wonder if I would ever land!

With a loud thump, I landed on my back in what appeared to be a field of tall weeds.

I tried to get up and walk but soon realized that my lower extremities didn't work. For whatever reason, I noticed that my boots were gone. The strange, euphoric feeling I had just felt a few minutes earlier was replaced by terror that welled up in me as I remembered the alligators and wild boar that frequented the natural lakes in this area! I listened intently, and I could hear something moving in the weeds off in the distance.

"Is this where I'll die?" I asked myself as I lay there on the damp, cool ground. My head was spinning, and I started thinking about my wife and my children. "What would they do without me?" I panicked. I thought about Andy, my oldest, who came to live with me when he was seven years old. His mother, whom I had never been married to, said that he was too unruly, and she thought he would be better off with his father. I gladly accepted her offer, and she put Andy on a plane. After a few years of hard work and discipline, Andy and I were finally very close. *What will he do without me?* I wondered. I thought of my youngest daughter, Denise, who couldn't wait for me to get home from work each day to buy her ice cream from the ice cream truck. My wife had a child from a previous relationship too, and I loved Nancy as my own child. I also had three other children named Sara, Berny, and Vicky, not to mention my beloved wife. *Will I ever see any of them again?* I wondered.

I didn't know much about God. My family had never attended church, but I believed there was a heaven and a hell. As I lay there, I asked God, "If I'm going to die now, why didn't You just take me at birth?" I had so many questions but no answers.

My mother told me how my father had raced to the emergency room at the hospital when she was in labor. He barely got the car parked before the nurse had my mother in a wheelchair, rushing her to labor and delivery. During the short elevator ride to the second floor, which seemed to have taken forever, my mother cried, "My baby is coming now!"

The nurse assured her that everything would be okay, and they would be at labor and delivery in just a minute. The elevator door sprung open, and the nurses were waiting. They quickly whisked her to a room and helped her into a gown. She cautiously climbed into bed, and the nurses made her as comfortable as possible. They told her that she should relax and that a nurse was going to examine her. The nurse pulled the curtain and lifted my mother's gown and the look on the nurse's face was complete panic!

The nurse screamed, "Get the doctor up here and get him now. This baby is coming!"

Another nurse said, "Would you like me to prep her?"

"No, there is no time for that!" she screeched. "Just get me a doctor. Any doctor on call! This is serious!" she wailed.

My mother asked with concern in her voice, "My baby is not due for at least two more months. Is everything going to be okay?"

The nurse said, "Just relax, honey. We are going to do the very best we can."

Just then the doctor burst into the room. Before the doctor could even get a word out of his mouth, the nurse said, "Oh, thank God you're here! She is crowning, and this baby is coming fast. She's two months early!" The doctor, still in his street clothes, barely had time to get his hands washed when the nurse handed him a mask. She held up a sterile surgical gown for him to slide his arms through. The doctor and nurse prepared for my arrival.

The doctor looked at one of the other nurses and said, "Make sure we have an incubator ready because this is a tiny one. We are going to need it!" At that very moment, I made my grand entrance into the world, although I'm not sure how grand it really was. The room did not erupt with joy. In fact, the mood was very somber. I wasn't making a sound or anything that resembled life. My mother thought to herself, *Oh, dear God, just let my baby live!*

The doctor gave me a swat on the behind like they did in those days, but there was no response. Again, he gave me another swat, and still no sound. The third swat was more brisk, and I let out a scream! The doctor held me up in the air and said, "A tiny, very tiny baby boy."

My mother pleaded, "Can I see him? Can I please see him just for a minute before you take him?"

The doctor agreed but said, "Just for a minute because this is a very critical time. He must stay warm and get oxygen."

After the nurses took me away, my mother began to question the doctor. Her mind raced with thoughts and questions. "Is he going to be okay?" she asked.

The doctor looked at her with a very serious look on his face and said, "I'm not sure, but if he makes it through the night, he will have a much better chance."

My mother did not get much sleep that night. Every time a nurse would pass her door or enter her room to check on her, she would ask the same question, "How is my baby?" Nurses would pacify her and say things like, "So far, so good. He's eating, and that's a good sign."

I don't believe any of them expected me to survive through the night. The nurses gathered around the incubator that would be my home for the next forty-five days of my life, and marveled at how tiny I was. Later that morning, my mother heard the doctor's voice coming from the nursery as he told a nurse, "I am amazed this baby survived through the night!"

My mother was ordered to stay in bed, but she could not contain herself. Against the doctor's orders, she got out of bed and met the doctor and nurse by the nursery. Relieved, she said, "He made it through the night!"

The doctor replied, "Yes, he did. He is quite a fighter!" As foolish as it may sound today, the doctor went on to say, "If he would have been a girl, I'm certain he would not have survived!"

My mother beamed with hope and excitement. She asked the doctor, "Do you think he is going to be okay now?"

The doctor said, "There are no guarantees, but with every day that passes, the chance of a favorable outcome greatly increases."

When I was born, medical technology was primitive compared to today's standards. There was no such thing as Life Flight, and doctors made no mention of transporting my tiny, frail body to a bigger hospital by ambulance. I don't believe they thought I would survive the trip. My mother spent most of her time staring through the glass into the nursery. But the first few crucial days quickly turned into a week, and then it was time for her to be released from the hospital.

My mother joined my father and my sister, Cindy, at home, where they lived in a small, two-bedroom apartment above my dad's mother, Melda. My mother made regular hospital visits to peer in the glass at the nursery almost every day. The following week it appeared that I was getting stronger, gaining a little weight, and had a very good chance of survival. However, my mother was not prepared for what she saw when she rounded the corner at the nursery during her next visit. My tiny body was lifeless and blue. She screamed and shouted, "Please help! Someone help my baby!"

Doctors and nurses came running and revived me. Once again, doctors told my mother it would be a miracle if her baby lived through the night. However, the Lord performed a miracle, and I, William Richmond, went home to join the rest of my family a month later.

It felt like I had been lying in the field, lost in thought for hours; however, I'm sure just a few minutes had actually passed. I knew I had to assess the situation, but I didn't have long. My right leg was barely hanging on. "Oh, God, I don't want to die. Please not like this!" I begged. I stretched my arms over my head and grabbed as many weeds as I could. I tried to pull myself on my back, but it was no use. I just couldn't do it. If I was going to get back to the side of the road, I would have to flip over onto my stomach. I attempted to turn over, but pain tormented every part of my body! Also, as I began to turn, my legs would not move, and I was getting weaker by the second.

I had one last option, but it would be extremely painful. Plus I wasn't sure how much more pain I could endure without passing out. I bunched up the neck of my shirt and put it in my mouth to bite on it. I grabbed the back of my right leg with my right hand

and flipped my legs at the same time as I turned my upper body. I landed facedown as tears ran down my cheeks. I wasn't sure that I could make it out of there alive, but I knew that I wasn't going to give up that easily! I was in a position to drag myself through the field to find help when the pain began to subside. The chill from the night air left my body, and a warm, comforting feeling came over me. This was different than the euphoric feeling I had just before the accident. "Is this God?" I asked myself. Then it hit me like a ton of bricks. *How could this be God? My family never went to church!* My mind began to wander. I remembered that as a teenager during a street festival in my hometown, a man tried to give me a Bible tract, and I said, "No, thank you. I'm an atheist." *Why would God want to help me now?* I thought to myself. This warm comforting feeling could only mean one thing. I was dying!

I pushed the terrifying thought away as I listened intently to see if there was a wild animal anywhere nearby. I didn't hear any wild animals, but I did hear a passing car, which helped me pinpoint the direction of the road. Tears began to run down my face again. *I'm alone. I don't have anyone to count on!* I thought to myself. In a panic, I pulled at the weeds and dug my fingernails into the soft, cool earth to move myself toward the direction of the passing car. After a good hard pull, I moved only inches through the field. At this rate, I certainly wouldn't reach the road alive. Time was crucial. I was fading fast, and it would take every bit of inner strength I had to get to the road. I raised my upper body into a pushup position and lunged forward over and over again as my limp and lifeless legs dragged behind me. I was sure I was paralyzed from the waist down. "I have to make it to the road to flag down a car," I told mysel as adrenaline raced through my body. After a few more lunges, I emerged from the weeds to the side of the road, exhausted! *Someone will have to see me lying here and stop*, I thought to myself.

Within a few minutes of reaching the edge of the road, I could hear a car approaching. I focused on the white line on the side of the road. *Not too close that I'll get run over again, but close enough that they will see me*, I thought. I got into position—up on my elbow, waving my other hand in the air the best I could. The car engine began to sound softer, and the car began to slow down. I thought to myself, *Surely, they had seen me! Help is here!* However, I was wrong. The driver rolled up to take a look and then stepped on the gas and sped away! I lowered myself facedown on the side of the road and began to sob. My mind raced. *Two people in the same night left me to die. First, the person who hit me, and now this!* I was sure I would die on the side of the road, and it never occurred to me to pray. I was too weak to pick up my head when I heard the next car approaching. I was lying facedown, but I picked my arm up as high as I could. To my surprise, the car came to a screeching halt!

A man jumped out of the car with a cell phone, one of the old-fashioned ones that looked like a walky-talky, and he called for help while his wife came to comfort me. "Try to relax. The ambulance will be here soon!" she said.

After her husband was finished talking on the cell phone, I asked him if I could use it to call my wife. "Would you like me to dial it for you?" he asked. I shook my head and gave him the number. When Shelly answered the phone, I had just enough energy to say, "I've been hit by a car. I don't know if I will live or not, but I want you and the children to know how much I love all of you!" I heard sirens blaring just as I handed the phone back to the owner so he could give Shelly the rest of the details.

Before long, red and blue lights were lighting up the night sky. There were police cars and an ambulance. As I was drifting in and out of consciousness, I could hear even more sirens in the distance. Just as the ambulance came to a screeching halt, the back doors sprang open. Paramedics put a tourniquet on my leg, placed me on a backboard, and one of the police officers began to take charge. He was on his radio calling for other officers to block the highway. Then the officer turned to me and asked, "Have you been drinking?" I shook my head to say yes. The officer immediately placed a breathalyzer in my mouth to measure my blood alcohol. The paramedics didn't waste any time calling for Life Flight. I was covered with a blanket and an oxygen mask was placed on my face. I was lying on the side of the road, clinging to life when a helicopter landed on the highway and the Life Flight paramedics took over. The ambulance paramedic met the Life Flight attendant and shouted, "Hit and run! It's a bad one. It knocked him right out of his boots!" As they lifted me onto a gurney, they worked like a finely oiled machine. They quickly strapped me down, and we were off to the local trauma center.

Once in the helicopter, I heard the attendant said, "Stay with me. We'll be there soon!" He turned to the other attendant and said, "He is going in and out of shock!" A few minutes later, he yelled, "I am losing him! Stay with me. We are almost there!" It sounded like I was in a tunnel and everyone's voices were far away. The sound of the helicopter's blades cutting through the night sky was growing faint.

CHAPTER 2

Praise be to the God and Father of our Lord Jesus
Christ, the Father of compassion and the God of
all comfort, who comforts us in all our troubles, so
that we can comfort those in any trouble with the
comfort we ourselves have received from God.

—1 Corinthians 1:3–4

A S MY MIND began to clear, the next thing I remembered
was lying on a gurney in the emergency room. I was sure
it was the expertise of the Life Flight attendants that saved my
life. As I lay there trying to remember some of the details of the
flight, a doctor handed me a clipboard and simply asked, "Can
you sign this?"

"What am I signing?" I asked.

"I need permission to amputate your leg," he stated
matter-of-factly.

I'm not sure if it was the shock of what he said or the way he
said it that made me shout out defiantly, "I want proof!" Calmly,
he turned around and walked out of the room.

He came back a few seconds later with a needle. Without
a word, the doctor pricked my right heel and leg. I couldn't do
anything but stare in disbelief! "Can you feel anything?" he asked

solemnly. Still in shock, I slowly shook my head from side to side to say no.

I am not sure if it was the drugs they were pumping through my veins, the remaining alcohol that was in my system, or if I was still in shock, but I blurted out, "Do whatever you have to do. I want to live!"

He looked at me very seriously and said, "There is no choice, and we don't have much time." I hung my head and signed the paper.

I was immediately taken to surgery, and I was in surgery for eleven intense hours. During the lengthy surgery, doctors amputated my right leg below the knee. They also attached two external fixators. One held my battered pelvis together where it had been broken in five places. The other one held my left leg together where it had been shattered in eighteen places below the knee.

The doctors did not have much hope that the amputation would heal. Sure enough, it did not. I was back in surgery a couple days later, and the doctors had to amputate my leg above the knee.

As I was coming out of surgery, I tried to focus on something familiar. As I looked around the room, I noticed my wife quietly standing there. Later I learned that Shelly spent almost an entire week at the hospital, nearly every day and night. She met with doctors regularly, but she spent most of her time at my bedside.

My dad and sister, Cindy, finally arrived from out of state just as I was placed into the intensive care unit (ICU). Only two family members could visit me at a time. Shelly informed me that she was going to get something to eat so that my dad and sister could spend some time with me. I was glad they were there, but I wasn't sure how much strength I had left to visit with them. As they approached my bedside, the look on my sister's face was pure shock, and my dad was stunned! Dad was usually not at a loss for words, but it took him a minute or two to get himself together enough to say in the strongest voice he could muster, "How are you doing, kid?"

I snapped back, "Much better if I could get out of this army hospital! Look at this place with beds lined up. They're even torturing a guy down there!" I pointed to the other side of the room.

"Billy, this is the ICU, not an army hospital. You were struck by a car!" he reminded me.

"I don't know why I was brought here," I continued.

"You are hurt really bad, but they're taking good care of you," he said calmly as he tried to reason with me. I was too confused from the drugs and the surgery to make any sense of it. As far as I was concerned, I was in an army hospital! Actually, I had never even been in the army, but for whatever reason, this was what I thought one would be like!

I quickly lost track of time. Day would turn into night, and Shelly and my family would take turns sitting at my side as I continued to hallucinate and talk nonsense from the strong painkillers they pumped into my system.

After a few days, the hallucinations subsided a little bit, but I still was not making any sense when I would try to communicate. Sometimes I was certain that I could walk. I would try to get out of bed. The alarm would sound, and the night-shift nurse, whom I nicknamed "Nurse Ratchet," would come running. After a few episodes, Nurse Ratchet threatened to tie me down. I was convinced that she was an army nurse and that she would do exactly as she promised, but that didn't stop me from driving her crazy with the call bell!

I was determined to get up and go smoke a cigarette, but Shelly was able to convince me that the red light on the device that measured my oxygen was a cigarette. I looked at the small red light that was clipped on the end of my index finger, and thought to myself, *Why not?* I held my fingers together as if I was holding a cigarette, put the make-believe cigarette up to my mouth, and inhaled deeply before exhaling. I chuckled at the fact that I was smoking a pretend cigarette, but the high levels of morphine made it seem almost euphoric. In a few days, I would be moved to a step-down unit.

As soon as they transferred me to my room, my mother arrived from Arizona; and surprisingly, I wasn't excited to see her. It was almost more than I could bear for her to see me like this. My room was getting full. My dad, my sister, and my wife were there, and a few minutes later, my mom came in. She reacted in the way I knew she would, and tears began to roll down her face. Cindy held Mom's hand and consoled her. She recommended that they go downstairs to get a cup of coffee. At the time, my mom was holding my hand with the most pitiful look that I had ever seen on a person's face. She struggled to mouth the words, "I love you!" My sister pulled on Mom's arm, and they rushed off to the cafeteria.

Dad tried to downplay the situation, and he said, "You're getting grizzly. Why don't you let me shave you?" One of my dad's pet peeves was an unshaven man, and I certainly was not in any condition to argue.

"Sure, go ahead," I quietly said. So the next time the nurse came into my room, Dad asked, "Do you have a pan of water, shaving cream, and a razor so I can shave my son?" The nurse gathered up the supplies and gently placed them on the bedside table. Dad began to carefully shave my face until every last hair was gone. "How does that feel?" he asked.

"Much better!" I exclaimed. Dad's eyes began to get watery. I had only seen this look one other time, and that was when my grandmother died. He quickly turned to make his way out of my room, so I wouldn't have to see him cry. Just as he made it to the door, he was met by my mom and my sister coming back from the cafeteria.

They stepped aside as Dad went charging through the door out into the hallway. He wanted to be left alone, but my mom and sister followed him. I heard Mom ask, "Are you okay, Ross?" There wasn't any answer. Mom hugged Dad for the first time in more than thirty years since their divorce when I was only two. "He's going to be okay," she stated as she tried to console him. Dad wasn't buying it, and he seemed to be in the middle of a complete breakdown. "Should I go get someone?" Shelly asked as she peered around the door. "No! I'm okay," Dad quickly responded. Then Mom, Dad, and my sister went to a sitting area at the end of the hall where they could talk. While they were out of the room, I began to think about the time I was reunited with my dad after their divorce.

When I was nineteen, my friend Pete and I were at the annual street festival held in my hometown. Pete and I were leaning against the front of the pool hall, drunk as could be, when a seemingly nice, well-dressed lady with lots of diamond jewelry walked up to me and said, "I'm your dad's wife, Betsy. Here's our address. Your dad would really like to meet you."

After she left, I looked at Pete and said with disgust, "He knows where to find me." Pete grew up with very difficult circumstances as well, and he was the one person who understood where I was coming from. Pete and I were truly best friends. I was certain that he would give me his best advice, and I valued his opinion for he always seemed to be the voice of reason.

I was surprised when he said, "I think you should go see him. I'll go with you if you want." That wasn't what I expected, but I agreed to think about it. A few days later, I took Pete up on his offer, and we were off on a journey to the other side of town to meet my biological father.

It was time to meet the man I had wondered about for the last nineteen years. We walked down the street, passing the football field and then the tennis courts without muttering a word. Pete looked over at me and said, "Are you okay? Are you sure you want to do this? I have never heard you silent for this long since I have known you." Pete was right. I usually had something to say about almost every situation! I was never one for mincing words. Pete could sense my apprehension. He knew me like a brother.

I replied, "I'm sure I want to keep going, but I'm just thinking about how awkward it will be. What if his wife was wrong and he really doesn't want to meet me? What if he's a real jerk and tells us to leave?"

Pete said, "I don't think that will happen, but if it does, we will give him a piece of our minds and leave. At least you won't have to wonder anymore."

"I guess you're right," I replied. Pete wasn't only the voice of reason, but he was also a hothead. If things turn bad, Lord only knows what he might say or do! However, it was a gamble worth taking because I knew Pete had my back and would support any decision I made. I didn't even know what I might say or do myself. My mind raced. I had so many questions, and there was so much I wanted to say.

Pete gave me my space and let me sort out my thoughts. Since I did ask him to come with me, I valued his opinion, and it would have been rude not to include him. I looked at Pete and said, "I'm not sure if we should be doing this. Maybe some things are better left alone."

"I don't think that would be a good idea. It would just leave too many unanswered questions," Pete said. "We've had too many conversations over the years about why."

"That is the looming question, isn't it?" I stated. My voice rose as I exclaimed, "Should I walk in his home and assume that he knows who I am with a barrage of questions beginning with why? Why did you sign the adoption papers as if you were giving away a puppy? Why did you let me live in such deplorable conditions? Why didn't you come looking for me?" I snapped. I was instantly remorseful for the way I was acting and quickly responded, "Sorry, Pete. I didn't mean to take it out on you."

"No offense taken!" Pete said. Pete knew that I wasn't doing well and said, "Why don't we sit down for a minute. I'm getting tired anyway."

I looked around and was somewhat confused. I said, "I know my eyes are bad, but I'm not seeing any benches!"

Pete chuckled and said, "Right here on the ground!"

We sat down on the tree lawn of a cemetery. I sat cross-legged with my thumb on my cheek and my pointer finger on my temple. I was deep in thought. I looked up a few minutes later and stated, "This is much more difficult than I anticipated."

Pete responded, "If I were in your shoes, I don't know what I would do, but I believe you owe it to yourself to at least find out what kind of a person he is. I do think if you give it a chance, you will get some answers to your questions."

"You're probably right, but I am not sure the questions are the end game."

Pete had a puzzled look on his face and said, "Do you mind explaining because I don't get it?"

I said, "I have never told anyone this before, so don't think I am nuts or anything, but I have this gnawing feeling in my gut. It feels like I am chasing something I just can't quite reach."

"Do you think meeting your father will resolve it?" Pete asked.

"I don't know. I have had this feeling before, and every time I think it is gone, it always comes back. It's not like I hear voices or anything like that. It's more like a feeling I get almost like I am not good enough at anything. I sometimes ask myself why this person or that person would want to hang around with me or why a pretty girl would like me."

"Now you are talking crazy!" Pete raised his voice.

"No, I am serious. We are not pillars of the community, but we are not that bad. The only ones we hurt are ourselves. I guess I am just feeling sorry for myself."

"Well, knock it off, and let's go meet your father!" We pulled ourselves off the grass and continued on our journey.

Before long, we were approaching my dad's street. As we rounded the corner, I couldn't help but notice that it was a nice upper-middle-class neighborhood. It was the fall of 1977, and nearly everyone on the street was outside either raking leaves or finishing projects before winter. Looking at these houses, I marveled at the new cars in almost every driveway! "Pretty nice neighborhood!" Pete exclaimed.

"Yeah, too bad the people aren't as nice as the neighborhood," I replied.

"What do you mean?" Pete asked.

"They think they're better than we are, and they won't even look at us," I said with a smirk. Pete waved at the next person we saw and said, "Hi, how are you?"

Just as I expected, the man turned his head like we were invisible. "See! I told you so!" I shouted.

Pete said, "You worry too much! They put their pants on just like we do—one leg at a time. If the truth be known, they probably have more skeletons in their closet than we do."

"Well, at least they have a closet!" I said and chuckled. "Besides, look at me. I don't belong in this neighborhood. I have bloodshot eyes from being drunk last night, tattered blue jeans, a torn shirt, and a floppy leather hat to cover my greasy hair that went out of style a decade ago!"

"Well, you'd better start fitting in because we are here!" said Pete.

"So we are." I groaned.

Pete and I stood in front of the house for a minute to size up the situation. I looked at Pete, shook my head, and said, "I don't think we should be here."

"We have come too far to chicken out now."

"Look at that car in the driveway. You could be driving it!"

"Don't you think I should get a driver's license first?" I scoffed. "I am nineteen years old and have never driven a car!"

"That might be for the best!" Pete joked.

"You're probably right."

After a few more seconds, Pete finally said, "Come on,. It's now or never."

"Okay, let's go." I said, but the truth was that I wanted to run in the other direction. My stomach was queasy, and I was sure if anyone answered the door, I would throw up all over them. I told Pete that we should go to the back door. "I'm sure they wouldn't want the neighbors to see us knocking on the front door!"

Pete scoffed and said, "Very funny." But he agreed, and we headed to the back door.

As we walked up the driveway, I quickly scanned the area. The car Pete mentioned earlier was a very new Pontiac Trans Am. In front of that was a two-car garage, and next to that was a pool with a deck around it. We stood next to the permanent gas grill in front of the screened-in patio. I stepped up to the door with a knot in my stomach and sweaty hands and gave the door a light knock. To my surprise, there was no answer. I looked at Pete and said, "See! There isn't anyone home, so we should go!"

Pete said, "Nice try. But let me show you how it is done." He muscled his way in front of me and gave the door about three good hard knocks!

Sure enough, a voice from inside shouted, "Come in!"

We walked through the screened-in patio, into the house, and up a couple of steps into the kitchen. There was the well-dressed lady we had met at the street festival, and she wore diamonds on every finger. She was sitting at the table, sipping coffee in a red bathrobe, and puffing on a cigarette like it was the last one she would ever get. "Oh, hi, I'm glad you're here," the woman said. "Have a seat and let me get you boys some coffee. I seemed to have forgotten your name," she stated as she looked at Pete.

With a smile, he said, "My name is Pete."

"That's right," she said. "Well, my name is Betsy in case you don't remember. Make yourselves comfortable. Your dad will be here soon. He had a small job to do this morning. I'm going to go get dressed." Pete pulled out a pack of cigarettes and packed them firmly by tapping the pack against his hand. He held out the pack and offered me a cigarette. I thought to myself, *Betsy puffed down three of them in no time!* I gladly accepted Pete's offer just as Betsy came walking into the room.

She looked surprised and said, "Oh, I didn't even know that you boys smoke!"

"Every now and then," I replied. But the truth was I smoked cigarettes and anything else I could get my hands on!

Just as we were putting our cigarettes out in the ashtray on the table, Betsy looked out the window and said, "Here comes your dad now." She had a disgusted look on her face and said, "I do wish he would get a new work truck! That thing looks terrible!" Pete shot Betsy a look. Lord only knows what he was thinking, but I'm pretty sure it had something to do with the fact that I would have been glad to have any old truck!

Pete and I didn't share the same opinion about the role or responsibility of my father. He thought that my father owed me something, but I didn't feel the same way. I'm not sure what it was I wanted, but it wasn't monetary. The three of us sat at the table in almost dead silence. Betsy looked out the window with anticipation. Pete looked mad, and I was just trying to overcome the sick feeling in my stomach. *Ready or not, here he comes!* I thought to myself as my stomach churned. A few seconds later, the door sprang open, and up the steps came the man I had wondered so much about.

My mind raced with thoughts. *What should I call him? Would it be his first name, Ross, or maybe Dad, or should I just say hello?* He saved me from making a decision. He walked in, looked right at me, and said, "How are you, kid?"

I responded, "I'm okay." I really wasn't okay. I had more thoughts going through my mind than I could possibly process. *What did he mean by kid?* I wondered. *Was he acknowledging me as his son, or was it just something he said?* I wasn't sure, but I liked the way it sounded.

After a brief moment, Betsy broke the silence and said, "This is Billy's friend, Pete."

My father extended his hand for a handshake and said, "How are you?"

Pete nodded his head and responded, "Okay." But I could tell that Pete was very uncomfortable with all of this.

Betsy poured her husband a cup of coffee and said, "When you're done with your coffee, why don't you show Pete and Billy around?"

Ross declined and said, "When I finish my coffee, I am going to get washed up. Why don't you show them the house, and when I get done, I will take them out to the garage."

Betsy started by saying, "You've already seen the kitchen."

We sure have! I thought to myself. I noticed the hardwood table with chairs that match, carpet on the floor, a built-in oven and stovetop, and a nice view to the pool. I don't think Pete was up for a tour. The look on his face said, "I've seen plenty, and I don't like it!" However, Pete accepted Betsy's offer because I believe he felt it was a better option than making small talk with Ross in case he finished early in the bathroom.

So the tour began with the living room. It was decorated in black and red with a Spanish American look. The room had black leather upholstered furniture, a fireplace, and a state-of-the-art TV and sound system. The bedrooms were next. Much like the living room, nothing was out of place, and everything matched. As we were finishing our tour of the house, my father met us in the hall and said, "Are you ready to go outside?" I quickly accepted his offer, but Pete wasn't as excited as I was. However, he came along anyway.

First, we stopped to admire the brand-new Trans Am in the driveway. It was snow white with fancy pinstriping and T-tops with a big block V-8 engine under the hood. "I just got it about a month ago right off of the showroom floor," my father said, beaming. "Last week I had it up to 135 miles per hour on the highway!" he boasted. Next, we went into the garage. One side was a bay for the car, and the other was a workshop with tools of every kind. We left the garage, and my father strolled over by the pool and said, "It's heated, and it even has lights in it!" By this time Pete's face was getting red. I could tell he was ready to explode at any second.

Pete leaned over and said, "He isn't doing anything but boasting and bragging about what he has. He should be ashamed of himself. He didn't give you anything as you were growing up. I don't know how much more of this nonsense I can take. It makes me sick!"

Just then my father said the magic words, "Let's go down in the basement, and we can play a game of pool and have a drink." I knew the right thing to do would be to leave and get Pete out of there. He was even more of a hothead when he had a couple of drinks! However, I couldn't force myself to leave. I wanted to be close to my father. I wanted to know him, and at the same time, I wanted him to regret not getting to know me when I was a child.

We went down about six or eight steps into the basement, which was equally as nice as the rest of the house. It contained a regulation-size pool table, another state-of-the-art sound system, and a fully stocked bar. My father walked over to the bar and said, "What will it be?" Pete chose whiskey and cola. My father chose whiskey and water, and I declined the offer. As much as I would have liked to have a drink, I knew someone had to keep a clear head. My father took a sip of his whiskey, looked at me, and said, "Go ahead. Rack the balls and let me see what you got!" As I racked the balls, he chose his favorite pool cue from the rack on the wall. Before he took his break shot, he walked around the table, stuck his hand into the side pocket, and pulled a yellow envelope out. He opened the envelope and counted twenty-seven hundred-dollar bills, returned the bills to the envelope, and then stuck the envelope full of money into his pocket. Pete was glaring at my father with his nostrils flaring, and my father glared right back and said, "No one gave Betsy and me anything. We worked hard for everything we have!"

Pete snapped and said, "It's too bad you didn't work as hard to put a coat on the back of your son, a roof over his head, a pair of shoes on his feet, or even a warm meal in his stomach!"

"You don't know what you are talking about!" my father rebutted.

With fire in his eyes, Pete said, "I know plenty. I was there when he was hungry and cold. How could any man live in the same town as his own son and let him live in such horrible conditions?" Pete wasn't holding anything back. "You didn't do anything to improve his life! You make me sick! How can you even call yourself a man?" Pete went too far. He attacked my father's manhood.

Dad slammed his pool stick onto the pool table and said to Pete, "You'd better leave before I throw you out!"

Pete fired right back by saying, "I wouldn't try that if I were you, but I will leave on my own! You don't ever have to worry about me darkening your doorway again! Your car, your house, your money, and especially your character don't impress me!" Pete bellowed. He turned and said, "I'll be at the corner bar."

I nodded my head and said, "I will catch up with you later."

As he stomped up the steps and slammed the door, Pete said, "Whatever!"

Dad turned to me and said, "What kind of friends do you have?"

I exclaimed, "Don't expect me to disregard Pete's loyal friendship! Pete was there when I was hungry and cold and when I had to wear the same clothes for a week at a time because I didn't have anything else to wear. In fact, his situation wasn't any better! Pete and I formed a bond by sharing our limited resources to survive. He is more like a brother than a friend! If you want me to leave, I will."

"If I wanted you to leave, I would have told you to leave with your friend!" he grumbled. I could tell by the look on his face he was getting uncomfortable with the conversation. Suddenly, he said, "Are we going to play pool, or are we going to talk all night?"

He broke the balls, and to my surprise, nothing went in! It was my shot, but I could hardly concentrate on the game. All I could think about was how much I wanted to win and make him proud of me. I knew Pete was right. As a matter of fact, I should be angry at the man who gave me away as a baby without a second thought. I just didn't feel angry, and more than anything, I wanted to get to know him. *Will getting to know my father finely get rid of the feeling of loneliness, hopelessness, and despair I feel deep in my gut?* I wondered.

We played four or five games of pool, and I didn't win any of them! I found out later that my father was a semipro in his younger days. The time at my father's house was winding down, but before I left, there was one question I had to ask. I wasn't sure how I was going ask it, so I just blurted it out. "So what do you want me to call you? Should I call you Ross, or would you prefer something else?" I wanted to call him Dad, but I couldn't take that chance in case he rejected me. I sensed that we both wanted to say something, but neither one of us could say it. I spoke first and said, "I could call you by your first name, but that seems a little rude," I said.

"Yes, I think so too." he said.

His face lit up, and his eyes sparkled as if he was having some sort of an epiphany, and said, "How about Dad? Are you okay with that?" he asked.

I felt myself getting emotional. I wanted to sob, but I was able to hold back the tears, shake my head, and say, "Yes, that would be fine."

I was getting anxious to meet Pete at the bar, and I sensed that my dad had other things to do, so I said, "I guess I should be going now."

However, Dad spoke up and said, "Why don't you stay for dinner?"

"Okay," I quickly accepted.

After dinner, Betsy cleared the table and started pouring coffee. She said, "Would you like some coffee, Billy?"

"No, thank you. I am going to be leaving soon," I said.

"Do you need a ride somewhere?" Betsy asked. "Your dad could drop you off."

"If it wouldn't be any trouble, I would like to go to the Chatter Box," I said.

We took the Trans Am for the ride to the corner bar in town. Of course, my dad squealed the tires around every turn and broke every speed limit getting there! I smiled and thought to myself, *This may be the nicest car I have ever ridden in.* The real excitement came when we arrived. I don't know if I was more excited about my friends seeing me getting dropped off in the Trans Am or if the high point was getting out of the car and saying, "I'll see you later, Dad!"

He replied by saying, "Goodbye, Billy! I hope to see you soon."

As the years went by, my dad and I actually became very close. I found it very comforting to have him near during my recovery after my accident. The days went by quickly in the hospital. The hallucinations stopped, and the doctors lowered the amount of medication; however, I was still confused, and my thoughts were fuzzy. I looked at my wife and could see the pain on her face. I wasn't too out of it to know that I had caused my family all of this grief. I wanted to cry so badly, but I didn't for fear of hurting my family even more. "Your mom, dad, and sister are at the end of the hall talking, and I'm going to see if they want to go and get something to eat. Why don't you get some rest? We will be back later," Shelly said.

While my family was gone, I drifted in and out of sleep. All of a sudden, I noticed a familiar face over my bed. It was Donnie, my adopted father with his new wife. Donnie had adopted me when I was four years old, shortly after my mother and he were married. "How long have you been standing there?" I asked.

"Just a few minutes," he replied. Like the rest of my family, Donnie didn't have much to say. Finally, he said, "We are going to be leaving soon." I closed my eyes, so it would be sooner rather than later. As hurt as I was, I still resented Donnie for what he did to my mother. I couldn't help but think about the conversation I had with Mom when she returned from a vacation. While she was on vacation, Donnie moved their RV to another woman's house. He had been seeing her on the side, and he left my mother with just the clothes on her back. After returning, my mother went to work as a cook in a restaurant/bar, making minimum wage. She called to give me the news. I was sickened by Donnie's actions. *My mother was the primary breadwinner in the family for most of their twenty-nine years of marriage, and this is the thanks she gets?* I thought as anger raged inside of me. She was sobbing uncontrollably as she said, "He took everything—the fifth-wheel, my clothes, pictures, everything. It's all gone!" she wailed.

"Donnie and I had our share of battles over the years, but this was even lower than I thought he would go," I said to myself as I drifted off to sleep.

My family returned from dinner to say good night before they went back to the motel. However, they were back bright and early the next morning. I had been moved to a regular room down the hall from the step-down unit. It was a huge room with two beds. Mine was closest to the window, and the other bed was unoccupied. "What a nice room!" Shelly said as my family came through the door. It had been nearly two weeks, and it appeared that I had survived the accident.

It was time for my sister and dad to return home. Just as they were saying their goodbyes, I couldn't believe who walked through the door next. It was my Uncle Lenny! "How did you get here?" I asked.

"I hitchhiked from the nursing home," he replied.

"That is almost a thousand miles away!" I shouted.

"I made it in three days," he said with a twinkle in his eyes. A preacher had picked him up and had gone out of his way to bring Uncle Lenny to the hospital. The preacher was also in the room and asked if he could pray over me. I gladly shook my head to say yes! As the preacher was praying, it occurred to me that no one had ever prayed for me before, at least not that I knew of. As soon as the prayer ended, Dad and Cindy shook hands with Uncle Lenny and the preacher and thanked them for coming before they left for the airport. The preacher left a short time later.

As soon as they left, Uncle Lenny didn't waste any time before asking, "Has that no-good brother of mine been here yet?" He was talking about Donnie. Uncle Lenny and my adopted father, Donnie, were brothers. I always liked Uncle Lenny much better.

"He was here yesterday with his new wife for about ten minutes, but I pretended I was sleeping so they would leave," I replied.

Uncle Lenny chuckled and said, "I know he's my brother and all, but that guy is just no-good. He never has been. Even as a child he was rotten." Uncle Lenny wasn't my uncle by blood, but he certainly was by love. For a moment, everything was quiet, and it was like there was an elephant in the room that no one wanted to acknowledge.

Finally, my mom blurted out, "Lenny, what are you doing in that hospital gown?"

"I ran out of colostomy supplies, and I had an accident. But they fixed me up downstairs in the emergency room," he replied.

Mom went on to ask, "So you don't have any clothes either?"

"Nope, just what's on my back," Lenny replied. In many ways, Uncle Lenny was like having a child around. He had a terrible automobile accident when he was younger, and he had suffered brain trauma.

"I'm going to the store to buy you some clothes," Mom said.

"Okay, Bonnie," Uncle Lenny replied. She wrote the sizes down and returned a short time later with some clothes.

"Here you go, Lenny. I got you some sweatpants and a T-shirt for now," Mom said. Uncle Lenny went and put his new clothes on right away. "I bought you a couple more outfits and some underclothes too," Mom stated.

"Well, thank you, Bonnie," Uncle Lenny said.

Mom told Uncle Lenny, "I'm going back to stay with the children so Shelly can stay here and work on getting Bill moved to a hospital closer to home. Would you mind coming along and giving me a hand?"

"Whatever you need, Bonnie," Uncle Lenny said, beaming. By now I was sure that Uncle Lenny had no plans of heading back to the nursing home and that he would be staying with us for quite some time!

The continuous IV drip that contained my pain medication was stopped and replaced with a morphine pump. "This will administer pain medication every six minutes as long as you push this button," the nurse said as she clipped the gadget onto the bed rail. Mom kissed me on the cheek and told me that she loved me before they made the hour-and-a-half trip back home. Shelly walked them to the parking lot, and by the time she came back, tears were running down my face from the pain! Shelly quickly found a nurse and brought her back to my room.

"Did you press the button?" the nurse asked as she placed my hand on it.

"No, I forgot!" I yelled. The nurse gave me a shot to relieve the pain and assured me that if I pressed the button, I could get pain medication every six minutes. As the pain subsided, I began to watch the clock on the wall at the end of my bed. I held the button in my hand so I wouldn't forget to press it every six minutes. Before long, the room began to spin, and I was pushing the button randomly. Of course, I could only get the medication as it was scheduled. I was back to slurring my words and slobbering on myself when I tried to talk. Shelly became concerned that I was overmedicating myself and told a nurse. Sure enough, later that night, the pump was lowered to reduce the amount of morphine that it could administer.

One day a young volunteer came to check on me, and to her surprise, I was hanging upside down from the triangular bar above my bed with my backside exposed from the open hospital gown! She screamed, and help came immediately to get me down. The pain medication was still making me a bit abnormal. What I wanted more than anything was a cigarette, and I was not going to fall for a pretend cigarette again. The guy next to me was getting a beer before every meal, and I couldn't even have a cigarette! One of the nurses said, "If you would concentrate on transferring from the bed to the wheelchair as much as you do complaining, you could go outside for some fresh air." That was all I needed to hear. Going outside meant I could smoke a cigarette!

Soon, a physical therapist came with a transfer board, and by evening I was transferring from the bed to the wheelchair like a pro. Shelly was even surprised, and like the nurse promised, she was able to take me outside, but not before we stopped at a fast-food restaurant on the first floor of the hospital. I ordered a burger and fries and gobbled them down before we got to the door. A man held the door open, and Shelly pushed my wheelchair out into the Florida sun. The air was brisk, and the sun was bright. I squinted and held my hand out for a cigarette. Shelly lit the cigarette and handed it to me, and I puffed it like it was the last one I would ever get. Since I had not had a cigarette in ten days, the sudden rush of nicotine into my system made my head spin and caused me to become extremely nauseous.

Shelly maneuvered my wheelchair through the crowded lobby to the elevator, where we returned to the fifth floor. Almost as soon as we returned to the room, a social worker came in to tell us that since I was doing so well, I could be transferred to a hospital closer to home. After the social worker left the room, Shelly said, "I'm so glad that you are moving closer to home. It will be easier for Mom and Uncle Lenny to come and see you, and I can come after work."

"It will be much easier on everyone," I replied.

"I'll bring the children up to see you when you get moved if you want me to," Shelly said.

"I don't think I am ready for that yet. I'm afraid that all of this hardware hanging out of my body will scare them."

"Just let me know when you're ready because they've been asking about you," she said.

"We'll start by talking on the phone."

"Okay, I am sure they will be excited to talk to you," she said.

I'm never going to be the same dad that I was, I thought sadly to myself. *Will I ever be able to walk my beautiful daughters down the aisle when they get married? Will I ever roughhouse with my sons again? What will they think of me?* It was too much to think about. Tears were running down my face, and my lips quivered as I looked at Shelly and asked, "What will they think of me?"

She replied, "They will love you just like they always have."

Shelly handed me a tissue to dry my eyes, and after a few minutes of silence, I randomly asked, "How do you think Mom and Uncle Lenny are doing? Do you think she's killed him yet?"

"Where did that come from?" Shelly asked with a chuckle.

"I don't know," I replied. "Uncle Lenny's a great guy. When I was a teenager, he tried to get a loan to buy me a new dirt bike!"

"He really loves you, doesn't he?" Shelly asked.

I shook my head yes with tears in my eyes again.

As the social worker promised, I would be transferred to a hospital closer to home a few days later. Shelly filled me in on the details of the move the night before. "I checked out of the motel today. I'm going to leave a little bit early and drive back home. Jill is going to drive me back up here in the morning so I can ride in the ambulance with you on the trip back tomorrow," Shelly said. Jill was Shelly's good friend.

"You don't have to do all of that," I replied.

"I want to. I love you!" she said as she stroked my greasy hair.

"Thank you. I love you too," I replied.

I began drifting off again, and Shelly kissed me as she was leaving. I opened my eyes just long enough to hear her say, "Get some rest, and I'll see you in the morning."

I slept most of the night, which was something I hadn't done in a while. The next morning shortly after breakfast was served, I heard the distinctive sound of Shelly's shoes coming down the hall. "Good morning! You're awake!" Shelly exclaimed. "Jill came up to see you before she has to drive back."

"How are you doing, Bill?" Jill asked.

"I've been better," I replied.

"I can see that," she said.

Shortly after Jill left to return home, I received some extra pain medication for the ambulance ride. I was already dozing off when the transport person showed up to strap me onto a gurney for the long journey to the hospital.

CHAPTER 3

The Lord will watch over your coming
and going both now and forevermore.

—Psalm 121:8

I FINALLY ARRIVED at our local hospital, which was about ten minutes from my home. This would be much easier for Shelly. As they checked me in, I saw that night was quickly approaching. Shelly said as she was preparing to leave. "I will be back after work tomorrow."

An hour or so later, I met my orthopedic specialist, Dr. Jack. He came into my room, introduced himself, and got right down to business. He unwrapped the bandage on my amputated leg and said, "They did a nice job with the amputation."

I could hear the Allen wrenches banging together, and I knew what that meant. He looked at the illuminated X-rays that were displayed on the wall as he stuck the wrench into the adjusting bolt on the external fixator that was holding my pelvis together. He said, "You know this is going to hurt, don't you?"

"Yes!" I said and winced.

"I'm so sorry, but I don't have any choice," he stated.

Once he was finished, I looked at Dr. Jack with tears running down my face and asked, "Can you sign an order so I can go to the smoking area?"

"Can you transfer from the bed to the chair on your own?" he asked. I shook my head again to say yes, and the nurse confirmed it. "Then I don't see why not," he said. The doctor walked out of the room, and I looked at the nurse with a stunned look on my face as if to say, "What's wrong with that guy?"

"I know his bedside manner isn't so good, but you will be glad you have him. He is one of the best in the business!" she exclaimed.

I had freedom to move about the hospital on my own, and I spent most of my time at the outdoor smoking area. I smoked a cigarette and went back to my room to call Shelly, so I could tell her about my newfound freedom. I dialed the phone, not realizing what time it was. She answered with a sleepy voice, "Hello?"

"Hi!" I said with excitement in my voice. "The doctor said that I could go to the smoking area any time that I wanted to!"

"That's great, but do you know what time it is?" she asked.

"No," I replied.

"It's after midnight, and I am exhausted. Can I call you in the morning?"

"I'm sorry. I didn't realize what time it was," I replied. After I hung up the phone, I began to wonder, *How can it be after midnight? It was only 9:00 p.m. when I went to the smoking area.* It occurred to me that I had fallen asleep in my wheelchair and lost track of time! That happened often because of the pain medication and even more than I realized.

My mom and Uncle Lenny showed up at the hospital bright and early the next morning, and we had a great visit. My mom wanted to let me know that she would be making the two-thousand-mile trip back home in a few days, and Uncle Lenny was going to stay so he could help Shelly when I came home from the hospital. My mother left the following week.

Uncle Lenny spent most days at the hospital with me, and

Shelly took him home with her when she came to the hospital after work. He was there every day, and Shelly was there every evening. I was facing one of the most challenging times in my life, but the small things that my family did out of love made it more tolerable. Uncle Lenny became so well known at the hospital that he would get a lunch menu just the same as I would. We played cards, ate cheeseburgers and French fries from the cafeteria, and watched game shows on television.

Sometimes we would reminisce about old times. I asked him if he remembered our trip on my motorcycle to visit his dad in a nursing home. Uncle Lenny replied, "Do I ever! You nearly killed me!"

About fifteen years earlier, I had made plans to visit a friend in the South. But things don't always work out the way we plan them, and this trip wasn't any different. My plan was to visit Uncle Lenny, his sister, and the rest of my adopted father's family before continuing on my journey. As I got closer to my destination, my bike didn't seem to be running right. The engine was misfiring, and it barely made it up the hill that led to their house.

Uncle Lenny told me of a man who lived nearby who worked on motorcycles and suggested that we take the bike there. We climbed onto my motorcycle, and I'm pretty sure we exceeded the weight limit. It was quite a sight! Uncle Lenny placed the half helmet on his head, which he referred to as a turtle shell, and straddled the bike. He weighed more than three hundred pounds! The entire family stood outside to watch our departure. I'm sure they didn't come out just to say goodbye. More than likely, some of them wanted to see if Uncle Lenny would really get on the little motorcycle. Others just wanted to laugh at how ridiculous we looked! I wondered if the bike had enough power to climb the steep hill that led to the main road. I pressed the button to start the motorcycle, and as it started, I yelled, "Hold on, Uncle Lenny!" I looked through the mirror at our audience, and some of them were pointing. Others were in a full belly laugh, and the rest were just covering their mouths.

Uncle Lenny's excess weight made the front wheel difficult to control on the gravel. After just a short time, I was fighting to keep the bike on the road. Eventually, I lost control, and we headed through a field, down a slight hill, and toward an area where a house had been torn down with just the basement left. Uncle Lenny grabbed onto my jacket for dear life. I stood on the foot pegs as if I was on a dirt bike, leaned hard to the left, yanked the handlebars, and just missed falling into the abandoned basement. We made it back onto the gravel road, and I asked Uncle Lenny if he was okay. He replied, "Every muscle in your body was tense, but you handled that pretty well. I had my feet down like skis, but I couldn't get off of the back of the seat because of this "chicken bar," as Uncle Lenny called it. He was referring to the backrest attached to the back of the seat.

By the time my bike was fixed, it was too late to go any farther. The family suggested that Uncle Lenny and I take a trip to visit the family's father at the nursing home. I agreed that it was a great idea, and once again, Uncle Lenny jumped on the motorcycle for the ten-mile journey. We made it there and back without any problems. When we returned, they were still laughing and carrying on about how funny Uncle Lenny looked with the turtle shell on his head. Uncle Lenny and I greeted the family with a laugh of our own! After dinner I said my goodbyes. It was great seeing everyone, especially Uncle Lenny, because he was my favorite.

This hospital stay was much more pleasant than the previous one. I certainly did not blame the hospital. After all, I was a very difficult patient. In fact, I didn't even blame Nurse Ratchet. I'm sure I was more of the problem than she was!

After a few days, I was beginning to settle down and get into some sort of a routine. I heard the familiar sound of Shelly's shoes just before she rounded the corner and entered my room. I perked up and said, "How are you doing today, babe?"

"I'm okay," she answered quietly. However, I could tell there was something else on her mind.

"What's bothering you?" I asked her.

"Is it that obvious?" she asked.

"Come on. What is it?" I asked.

"The children really need to hear from you," she said sadly.

"I know that I have been putting it off. I just feel like I have let all of you down, and I don't have any idea how to fix it." My voice began to crack. "Okay," I said as I cleared my throat. "Will you call and let them know so it won't be so much of a surprise?"

Shelly picked up the telephone and dialed the number. "Hi, Andy. Your dad wants to talk to you guys!" she said excitedly as she handed me the phone.

"How are you doing, Dad?" my oldest son asked.

"I'm okay. I hope I will be coming home soon," I replied.

"I hope so too!" he said anxiously. I heard him clear his throat to muster up the deepest twelve-year-old voice he could. "Don't you worry about anything because I have everything under control here," he stated in the most reassuring voice possible.

"You have turned into quite a young man while I've been in the hospital. Thank you for all you're doing," I said. "How about your grades in school? Are you keeping up with them?"

"I'm doing good in school," he replied.

"I love you, Andy, and I'm really proud of you," I said.

"Thank you, Dad. I love you too!" he replied. "Nancy wants to talk to you now."

"Okay, be good!" I said as I waited to hear Nancy's voice.

"Hi, Dad," she said. Nancy was the oldest child at home. Shelly had her from a previous relationship, but as far as I was concerned, she was my daughter too.

"Hi, Nancy! How are you?" I asked.

"I'm doing good. I've been helping Mom a lot. I even went to the store to buy groceries and made dinner a couple days ago."

"That's great!" I said with praise in my voice. "Thank you for helping your mom keep everything together and for looking out for your little sister," I said.

"You're welcome, Dad!" she exclaimed.

"You're turning into quite a fine young lady at fourteen years old. I'd better hurry up and get out of here before you are completely grown up."

"Thank you, Dad, but I'm sure you will be home in time to see me grow up," she replied. "Denise is jumping up and down, waiting to talk to you, so I'd better go and let her talk. I love you, Dad."

She handed Denise the phone, and I heard the voice of a little five-year-old angel say, "Hi, Daddy! I love you!"

"I love you too, honey!" I replied. "Are you being good?"

"Yep, I even helped Mom make my bed today," she said with eagerness.

"That's great!" I replied.

Then she exclaimed, "I drew you a picture. It's me and you, but I am holding you up because you only have one leg."

"You are going to be quite a good little helper!" I said with praise in my voice, but the comment ripped right through the very fabric of my being. "I'd better go for now. I am getting tired," I said.

"Okay, Daddy. I love you!" she said.

"I love you too, honey," I replied.

I heard her little voice say, "Goodbye, Daddy!" I handed Shelly the phone so she could hang it up. I tried to hold back the tears, but it was no use. I began to sob uncontrollably.

"What's wrong? It sounded like it went really well!" Shelley asked. I shook my head yes. I dried my eyes with a tissue, feeling angry with myself for crying.

After pulling myself together, I looked at Shelly and said, "I'm going to be a burden to someone for the rest of my life."

"What makes you say that?" Shelly asked. I told her about the picture Denise drew. "She is only five years old, and she loves you. I have known you since I have been fourteen, and I have never seen you give up on anything. Don't start now! We will get through this!" She rubbed my arm gently.

"I know. I am just having a moment!" I replied.

"I'm going to the smoking area for a cigarette. Do you want to go with me?" she asked.

"Sure", I replied.

I climbed into my wheelchair, and Shelly asked, "Do you want me to push you?"

"No, I got it," I replied. We sat at the smoking area for nearly an hour before returning to my room. "I'm getting tired," I said.

"Why don't you get back into bed? I'm going to be leaving soon," she replied. Shelly kissed me before leaving and said, "I know you are going to be okay." Shelly's optimism made me smile. "Good night. I will see you tomorrow," she said.

In what seemed like a short amount of time, I woke up to a familiar clicking sound. I rubbed my eyes and blinked a couple of times before noticing Uncle Lenny sitting next to me with a deck of cards in his hand. He was playing solitaire on my bedside table. "What time is it?" I asked with a groggy voice. "It's almost seven o'clock. You'd better get up before you miss breakfast!" he said. Uncle Lenny wasn't one for missing a meal if he could help it, and his waistline certainly showed it! Today was like many other days. Uncle Lenny and I ate breakfast, and then we went to the outdoor smoking area, so I could smoke while we played cards. We would make our way back to my room around lunchtime, where we would have the usual cheeseburgers and fries. After lunch I would fall asleep to the same sound I woke up to, Uncle Lenny playing cards.

After my nap Uncle Lenny was still playing! "You are going to wear the spots off of those cards," I said.

"That's okay because I have another deck in my pocket," he replied.

After watching him for a little while, I asked, "What are you playing?"

"Double Solitaire," he replied.

"I know I am a little bit confused, but there is only one of you," I said.

"I'm playing against a ghost man."

"I have been watching for a while now, and I haven't seen the ghost man win yet. Are you sure you are not cheating this ghost man?"

"Nope, he just isn't as good as I am," he said and smiled.

"Okay, if you say so," I replied. "Do you want to go down to the smoking area?"

"Sure, let me put my cards away," he replied.

We were at the smoking area when Shelly showed up. "I thought you would be here," she said and handed me a paper bag with a pack of cigarettes and a couple of candy bars. I could barely say, "Thank you," before she exclaimed, "I have something funny to tell you!" Laughter was in her voice. "Last night when I kissed you before I left, I knew right then that everything would be okay. When I was driving home last night, I started thinking about it and drove past our road. I was in such deep thought that I was two exits away before I realized it."

"That's funny!" I replied. Shelly's optimism was real and almost contagious. I also began to believe that everything would turn out just fine and our lives would only get better from this point on.

I even started to like Dr. Jack, and I believed he respected my determination. However, neither Shelly nor I expected what happened next. The following day as he entered my room, Dr. Jack stated, "I have some bad news for you. I am going to have to take you back into surgery to manipulate the bones in your leg." Just as I had been dreaming about going home, the news of more surgery was almost more than I could take.

The surgery went well, but it didn't eliminate the excruciating pain when additional adjustments had to be made to the external fixators. It was a setback, and they had to increade the pain medication again. It felt like I had been in the hospital forever, but it had only been about three weeks.

It was about a week before Christmas when I told Dr. Jack that I would like to go home to watch my children open their gifts at Christmas. "Let me see how you are doing in a few days, and I will let you know," he said. A few days later, Dr. Jack came in for his evening rounds when Shelly was there. He looked at her and said, "If you can make the necessary arrangements with home health and get the medical equipment Bill needs, I will let him go home for Christmas." He went on to say, "The hospital social worker will help you with anything you need."

"Okay. Thank you!" Shelly said with excitement in her voice. She went to work the next day a couple hours later so she could meet with the social worker. By the following day, everything was in place so I could go home for Christmas. Shelly was nearly skipping with joy when she came into my room for her nightly visit. "You are coming home for Christmas!" she announced with a smile from ear to ear!

I went home a couple days later and couldn't believe what my wife had accomplished in such a short amount of time. I had a hospital bed set up in the living room. Skilled nurses were scheduled to come in two times a day, and best of all, I had an electric wheelchair. "Well, what do you think?" Shelly asked with a giant smile on her face! "I wasn't sure what you would think about the wheelchair. If you don't like it, we can send it back."

"I think it's great!" I exclaimed. I was eager to transfer from the manual chair to the electric one and give it a try. She explained all of the buttons and how to navigate the chair. It even had a seat that would rise up with a push of a button, so I could reach things without standing up.

Before long, I was racing up and down the driveway with my new wheelchair and even around the neighborhood. Christmas was great, and the children received nice gifts, thanks to family and friends. Shelly and I even received gifts, including a Rottweiler puppy that she thought I needed.

Christmas came and went, but things didn't stay lighthearted for very long. I was admitted back to the hospital at the beginning of January with a staph infection. I stayed in the hospital for a couple more weeks, and Shelly did her best to make me as comfortable as possible. The next time she came to visit, she announced that she had a surprise. "Get in your wheelchair and come outside. I want to show it to you." She pushed me through the lobby to the outside pickup area. Then she pointed at a minivan. She had traded the Bronco in for a minivan. "I got it from your friend who owns the car lot," she stated. I couldn't quite figure out why she was so excited over a minivan until she opened the side door and pushed a button. A wheelchair ramp lowered to the ground. "Let me show you how it works!" she exclaimed. She climbed into the van and came driving out onto the ramp with my electric wheelchair and then lowered it to the ground. "I brought it for you!" she said as she drove it up next to the manual chair.

"That's great!" I said with a lump in my throat. I was sad to get rid of the Bronco, but I knew it was necessary.

For the next two weeks, I whizzed around the hallways, exploring the hospital and frequenting the smoking area in my fancy wheelchair, my Harley-Davidson vest hung over the back of it. It was finally time to be released from the hospital.

CHAPTER 4

Save me, O God, for the waters have come up
to my neck. I sink in the miry depths, where
there is no foothold. I have come into the deep
waters; the floods engulf me. I am worn out
calling for help; my throat is parched. My eyes
fail, looking for my God. But I pray to you, O
Lord, in the time of your favor; in your great love,
O God, answer me with your sure salvation.

—Psalm 69:1–3, 13

SHELLY DROVE ME to an infectious disease doctor day after
day for the next forty-five days. Day in and day out, the
routine was the same. Nurses came into our home two times a
day, and we would also make regular visits to Dr. Jack's office.
Shelly would go outside, open the side door of the minivan, and
press the button that lowered the wheelchair ramp to the ground.
"Come on. We're going to be late!" she shouted. I did not enjoy
taking the ride across town. That meant that I would have to
get up and get dressed, something that I preferred not to do. My
family was pitching in to do all that they could. The children
were absolutely amazing, and they were always willing to help.
Uncle Lenny told Shelly, "I don't get very much money in social
security, but you're welcome to have it."

Shelly was like a symphony conductor directing it all without missing a beat. I was grateful for my family, but I couldn't shake the depression that hung over my head like a dark, looming cloud. "Is this how I will live the rest of my life? Dependent on my family for everything?" I asked myself.

"Come on. We are going to be late!" I heard Shelly say for the second time.

"Okay, I'll be right there," I replied.

I maneuvered the wheelchair to the van, and Shelly said, "You look rough!" She really meant that I hadn't washed my face or combed my hair, and she was right. The ride to the doctor's office was quiet. I rode in the back of the van, and Shelly drove. I was deep in thought. I told myself that it was better when I was in the hospital. At least my family didn't have to wait on me.

We arrived at the doctor's office a short time later. The appointment went well, and I was released. I was free of the staph infection I had contracted in the hospital. This was the first of many hurdles to overcome, but I didn't find much comfort in it. After we left the doctor's office, Shelly asked, "Do you want to go to that little diner that you like?"

"Sure, if we can afford it," I replied, knowing that we couldn't. Shelly always came up with the money to pay for what I needed and usually what I wanted. I wasn't going to argue because the little diner gave me a slight feeling of something normal. We stopped in the parking lot near the door of the restaurant.

Shelly opened the side door of the van and lowered the ramp. "There you go," she said with a smile.

"What could possibly make her smile?" I asked myself. Shelly made sure the ramp was in place. I drove the wheelchair onto the platform, and she lowered me to the ground. She held the door so I could get into the restaurant.

All of the servers knew us by name. "How are you doing today, Bill?"

"Okay," I replied without making eye contact. Shelly hurried in front of me to help one of the servers move chairs out of the way so I could drive my wheelchair up to the table.

"Two coffees?" the lady asked. Shelly said yes, and I just shook my head to signal the same. After bringing our coffee back to the table, she asked, "The usual? Two eggs over medium, sausage, potatoes, and toast?"

"Sounds good," I said.

Shelly said, "I'll have the same thing."

"I'll put it right in for you," the server said. I didn't have much to say while we were waiting for our food. Shelly noticed the discontent on my face and stretched her arms crossed the table to hold my hand.

There wasn't much to say, but with a tear in my eye, I just said, "I'm sorry."

She clutched my hand tightly and said, "You don't have to be sorry about anything. You didn't do anything wrong."

"I'm just sorry that you have to go through all of this," I said.

"We are going to get through this together, but I am going to need your help," she replied. "One of the things that always attracted me to you is your strength, and I don't just mean your physical strength. You are the strongest person I have ever met, and I need you to be that person again."

I shook my head okay. I had to do a better job of hiding my emotions from Shelly. *She has enough to worry about,* I thought to myself. Sometimes I was angry, and sometimes I was worried or afraid. But most of the time, I was just depressed. I'm not sure how she accomplished all that she did, but I was grateful.

Shelly slept on the sofa in the living room next to my hospital bed so she could take care of me when I would wake up in the middle of the night. I would try to unwrap my leg, thinking that I was taking off my shoes. I didn't realize it at the time, but an accident or illness of this magnitude affects the whole family. My five-year-old daughter told the home health nurse that she wanted to be a nurse when she grew up so she could help people.

My son, who was twelve years old at the time, asked the owner of the market where Shelly worked for a job. "Aren't you going back to school soon?" the man asked.

"I'm not sure if I am going back to school. It's going to be a long time before my dad can work again. I really need a job to help my dad," Andy replied. Nancy cut her vacation short to come home and help her mother hold the family together.

I was still spending most of my time in the hospital bed. No matter how much I wanted to keep my emotions in check, I couldn't do it. I wanted to help my wife. I wanted to help my family, and I wanted to help myself. But the best I could do was just take another pain pill. Every time the medication would start to wear off, the same haunting thoughts would return. *I am nothing but a burden to my family.*

One day I confided in Shelly that I was extremely constipated. "That is a normal side effect of the pain medication," she said. "You should drink more water." By that evening after several glasses of water, I still wasn't having any luck. "Why don't you try some bran cereal?" Shelly asked.

"Okay, would you make me a bowl?" I asked. She brought the cereal to me shortly before everyone else went to bed. I wasn't eating much those days, but it tasted great. An hour or so later, Andy got up to use the bathroom, and I asked him, "Would you make me a bowl of bran cereal?"

"Sure, Dad," he replied. Later that night I asked Nancy the same question ... and then Uncle Lenny before I realized it I had eaten the entire box of cereal!

The next day the bran flakes started doing the job. I raced into the bathroom as fast as my wheelchair would go. After a while, I cried out, "Shelly! Call the doctor. There is something wrong with me."

Shelly came to the bathroom door to find out what the dilemma was. "What's wrong?" she asked.

"I've been in here forever, and I can't stop going to the bathroom!" I shouted.

"Well, you're not constipated anymore," she stated.

"No, but there is really something wrong. I know there is," I said frantically.

"Just wait a little bit, and if you are not feeling better in a little while, I will call," she assured me.

I returned to my hospital bed, convinced that I was likely going to die. After questioning the rest of the family, Shelly determined that I had eaten the whole box of cereal. She came to my bedside holding the empty cereal box, doing her best not to laugh. "You ate the whole box. It's no wonder you can't stop going to the bathroom!" she said with her hand covering her mouth. "I'm sure you are going to be okay," she assured me. I trusted her judgment, and eventually, I realized she was right.

Shelly tried to convince me to get up, but that was not going to happen. I preferred to stay in bed and nod in and out from the massive amount of pain pills my body became dependent on. I was convinced that I needed more and more pain pills until I eventually had myself in a drug-induced stupor, which would cause me to slobber on myself and slur my words. After waking up from a comatose state one day, my face was itching, and I asked Shelly for a bowl of water to shave. She refused, stomped to the bedroom, and said, "If you want to shave, you are going to have to get into your chair and go over to the sink." I was angry, but I later found out that she went into the bedroom to cry because she was worried that I was becoming bedridden and dependent on others. Shelly was coming to the end of her rope, but I was too messed up to know or even care.

As a desperate attempt to get me some help, she asked some friends of ours to come over to see me. Sure enough, a few days later, Ben and Peggy came over to visit. I never did know their last name. I just called Ben "Ben the dog catcher" because he worked for animal control. I'm not sure what was more surprising—Ben and his wife seeing the condition I was in or me when I saw Peggy break into prayer and Ben start talking in tongues. I wasn't sure about all the God stuff. They seemed serious about it, and it sounded as if they knew what they were talking about. But for me, I had more questions than answers.

I asked myself, "Where was God when my adopted father beat me violently? Where was God when I was a child and my parents would drop me off at a family member or friend's home for weeks at a time? Where was God when I had to sleep on the floor at people's homes, people I barely knew, covering up with coats from the hallway coatrack to stay warm?" I wasn't mad at God. I just didn't understand the concept. I closed my eyes, and Ben asked if I was tired. The truth was I had been reflecting on one of the worst beatings Donnie had ever given me.

The summer I turned ten years old, my parents and many of their friends met up at a house down the street every weekend. It was the most exciting event I had ever seen. We had barbecues and yard games, and there were motorcycles of every kind in the yard. On this particular day, the motorcycle pack took off on one of their rides. It sounded like thunder as they were tearing down the street! Their rides usually meant they were going from bar to bar, and they would come back more intoxicated than when they had left. This time was no different. Yard games soon became boring, and I told the other kids that the owner of the house said we could drive the go-kart if we could get it started. I jumped into the go-kart, and the other kids pushed me up and down the road. Before long, it started to rain. Just as we were making our way back to the house, I heard the thundering sound of approaching Harleys. One of the other children asked, "We're not going to get in trouble, are we?"

I said, "No, they said we could drive it if we could get it started." But was I ever wrong!

I could see the angry look on Donnie's face as he rolled by on his Harley. He screamed and said, "Get that thing back to the garage!" The other children helped me push the go-kart back to the garage, but we were puzzled.

"Why are we in trouble?" they asked. "They said we could drive it if we got it started."

As I walked back around the house, Donnie met me with his belt in his hand and said, "I know this was your idea, wasn't it?" I tried to explain that we had permission, but he wasn't hearing it. He pushed me toward the porch and began striking me with his belt. I thought to myself, *Someone's got to stop him! Where's my mother?* I am certain she would not let this go on. When he was finished, he picked me up off the ground by the arm and said, "If you ever do anything like that again, it will be worse next time."

I suffered unimaginable embarrassment and humiliation, but I dusted myself off and held my head up high. I refused to let it show. The other children were eager to console me, but I refused to shed a tear. The thing that puzzled me the most was why no one came to my aid and why my mother didn't stop him like she always had in the past. Just as I was replaying all of this in my head, my mother drove up in the blue Volkswagen. She wasn't there when the punishment took place. Donnie raced over to greet her as she drove up and explained that I had put myself and the other children in danger by fooling around with the go-kart. He had no choice but to give me a whipping. I didn't even try to rebut his nonsensical logic, but something happened that day. I was certain he would never make me cry again.

Ben's voice brought me back to the present as he said, "When you get out of this bed, I will take you fishing. I have a great spot where we can get your wheelchair right up to the water."

"That sounds great!" I said. I am not sure if it was the prayer, the thought of going fishing, or Shelly's encouragement, but a few days later, I got out of bed, shaved, and went outside.

My wife started to do less and less for me, and I began to do more for myself. The home health care nurse was thrilled at my improvement. From time to time, I would wonder what it would be like to walk again. I told myself, "If I was ever to walk again, I would have to strengthen the remaining part of my amputated leg." Day after day I would lay flat on my back in my hospital bed and push my amputated leg against the mattress, using it to elevate the rest of my body up off of the mattress in an attempt to strengthen my stump. The next time the nurse came for her regular visit, I held my stump in the air and said, "Put your hands right there and see how strong I am!" Then I pointed to the back of my leg. She did as I asked and placed her hands on my stump. I thrust it in a downward motion and sent her backing up across the room, stopping just short of going through the TV screen!

"Oh my! You are strong!" she cried out with a surprised look on her face.

I was still very unstable, and I had a hard time thinking clearly. Shelly told me that she was going to get rid of our waterbed and get a regular bed that would be easier for me to sleep in. I forgot about the conversation we had regarding the bed, and when the neighbors came over to get the waterbed, I had a meltdown. "Where are they going with our bed?" I asked Shelly. Before she could get a word out of her mouth, I cried out, "I knew this was going to happen. We will never sleep together again! What kind of a husband am I? I can't even sleep with my wife."

Shelly leaned over my wheelchair and wiped the tears from my eyes before consoling me with a hug. "Don't you remember we are going to get a bed that will be easier for you to sleep in?" she asked.

"I guess so," I replied. I still wasn't quite sure. In fact, I wasn't sure of anything. *Is she going to leave? I wonder if she will take the children*, I asked myself. It was too much to think about. I climbed into my hospital bed, took a few pain pills, and went to sleep.

When I woke up, Shelly was eager to show me something. "Get up, and come back to the bedroom. I want to show you something," she said with excitement in her voice. I gently transferred back to my wheelchair and made my way to the bedroom. My mouth gaped open, and I asked, "Where did you get that?" as I stared at a freshly made bed.

"I got the frame and the nightstands from the neighbor I gave the waterbed to. Your friend, Luis, brought the mattress set from his store, and you slept through it all," she said. "I thought maybe we could sleep in here together if you feel like it."

"Absolutely, but I'm afraid that you'll get hurt with all of this hardware hanging out of my body," I replied, referring to the external fixators.

"Don't worry. We will put pillows between us!" she exclaimed. For the first time in more than six months, my wife and I were sleeping in the same bed. I was lying in bed with my arm around my wife, holding her head tight to my chest. We talked and talked for the first time in a very long time, and I finally felt like there was a flicker of hope. My eyes were getting heavy, and Shelly said, "It looks like you are getting tired."

"I am," I said, but I wanted the moment to last forever. We kissed each other passionately, before turning in for the night.

"Everything you need is on the nightstand beside of you," Shelly said as I drifted off to sleep.

I woke up to the smell of sausage and coffee, and it seemed strange to wake up in a normal bed. Still in my nightclothes, I climbed into my wheelchair and made my way to the kitchen. "I didn't expect you up already. I'm making you breakfast, and I was going to bring it in when it's done," Shelly said.

"Thank you, but I'll eat out here," I replied as she set a cup of coffee in front of me at the table.

As time went by, I began to take less pain medication, but I was still running out long before it was time to get it refilled. I went to doctor after doctor, begging until I found one that would give me more pain pills. I continued to take less pills, but I was still was running out. Then the truth finally dawned on me. My wife was taking my pain pills too. I confronted her, and she actually admitted it! It was no longer a secret. We were both addicted and simply shared the pills. I was transitioning from a helpless invalid to a drug addict.

I rode around the neighborhood in my electric wheelchair. I went to the market where Shelly worked and to the local flea market with ease. My body was starting to heal, but my thoughts were still cloudy. My newfound freedom came with a price. Paranoia began to set in. I felt like a helpless target.

Shelly's friend Jill stopped over to see me. I was sitting in the bedroom alone. "I thought you would be outside," she said.

My lip began to quiver, and tears started running down my face as I sobbed and said, "Look at me! I couldn't defend myself if my life depended on it. I would be better off if I would have died!" I wailed, but the thoughts were just too strong, always the same. I was sure that I would be attacked and have no way to defend myself. Not all days were bad though, and when they were good, they were really good. I enjoyed talking to the neighbors, especially Ken, the elderly man next door. We were even planning a trip to a theme park on the other side of the state with Shelly's sister, Kim, and her husband, Mike.

I was sitting in the driveway when Kim, Mike, and their two children arrived. "Shelly, your sister is here!" I yelled. She raced out of the house to greet them. It had been a couple of years since Shelly had seen her sister. After she finished hugging Kim and Mike, it was my turn. We looked at each other for a minute as if no one knew what to say. I extended my hand for a handshake with Mike to break the awkward silence. "How are you doing, Mike?" I asked.

"Not too bad. How about yourself?" he asked.

"I'm okay," I said in the most reassuring voice I could find.

Kim hugged my neck and said, "I am glad you're doing better." After breakfast the next day, we were off on our trip. Shelly, the children, and I led the way in the wheelchair van, and Mike, Kim, and their children followed us.

We checked in at the hotel right cross the street from the

theme park. The children were jumping with excitement to go to the park and ride the rides. We gathered in front of the motel to wait for the shuttle that would take us there. A bus arrived, but a problem quickly presented itself. The bus was not wheelchair accessible. Shelly asked Mike, "Can you carry Bill onto the bus?"

"I'm not sure," he replied.

Shelly stepped in front of Mike and said, "Put your arms around my neck." I did as she asked, and she put one of her arms behind my back and the other arm under my legs and then hoisted me out of the wheelchair like an infant. Shelly used every bit of strength in her 120-pound body to carry me up the two steps of the bus and place me in the first available seat. Mike's eyes as were as big as dinner plates, and Kim's mouth was hanging open! They were amazed at Shelly's strength, and quite frankly, so was I! Without thinking twice, she climbed into my electric wheelchair, drove it into the motel, and came back out with a manual one. She hauled the wheelchair onto the bus and said, "Okay, we're ready now." When we arrived at the theme park, Shelly repeated the process, only in reverse, placing me in the manual chair.

Of course, there were some unseen benefits to being in a wheelchair. Our entire party was escorted to the front of every line. The day at the theme park was fun for all of us, and we spent the next day lounging around the pool. The children swam with Mike and Kim, while Shelly sat at a table near the pool. "Are you having fun?" Shelly asked with widened eyes.

"Oh, absolutely. This is great!" I replied, but I couldn't stop thinking about her carrying me like a baby. *What if she would have hurt her back?* I asked myself. Before my mind had long to wonder, the kids were getting out of the pool. The mini vacation would come to an end the next day.

On the way home, we stopped at a buffet to eat lunch. Andy and I had an eating contest, and we ate for a solid hour. The vacation was over, and we had returned home. I couldn't help but think about how much fun I had had. *I just hope my family had as much fun as I did*, I thought to myself. The week ended, and Mike, Kim, and their children packed up for the trip back home.

That night at bedtime, I held Shelly as I usually did with her head on my chest. I told her, "I hope you and the children had as much fun over the last week as I have." Shelly started to sniffle and wipe her eyes. "What's wrong?" I asked. She didn't answer. Again, I asked "Shelly, what's wrong?"

Reluctantly, she said, "I spent the bill money on our vacation. I just felt like we all needed it so badly." It was the first time I had seen my wife have a complete breakdown since the accident. Shelly was sobbing profusely, and all I could do was hold her tight and wipe the tears from her eyes like she had done for me so many times before.

"It's going to be okay. I will take care of it," I reassured her.

"What can you do?" she asked.

"I'm not sure, but we will take a look at the bills in the morning."

"Thank you. I have always depended on you for everything, but I just can't do this much longer," she said with a whimpering voice. Shelly went to the bathroom before we turned in for the night. She climbed back into bed and hugged me tightly and said, "Thanks for not being upset. I did the best I could."

"You did better than okay. You did great," I replied.

"It doesn't feel like it," she said. Once again, I assured her that everything would be okay, and we fell asleep a short time later.

Morning quickly approached, and the first thought that came to my mind as I was getting out of bed was, *How am I going to fix this delinquent bill situation? I can't let my wife and family down.* It was slightly after daylight when I rolled out to the table. Uncle Lenny was already up, playing solitaire, of course.

"How about a cup of coffee?" Uncle Lenny asked in a chipper voice.

"That sounds great," I replied. I sipped my coffee without much to say.

"What's bothering you?" Uncle Lenny asked.

"Last night Shelly told me that we were behind on the bills."
I was trying to figure out how much money we had coming
in compared to what we had going out. After questioning Uncle
Lenny, the numbers just didn't add up. "Uncle Lenny was giving
Shelly his social security check and just keeping enough money
to play bingo. Plus she had my check, and she was working forty
hours a week.

Shelly got up a short time later, and after she had some coffee
and breakfast, I asked to see the bills. I could tell Shelly didn't
want any part of it, but she did as I asked. After going over the bills
with her, I was convinced that we were two months late on our
rent for the house, and the electric was due to be turned off any
day. Shelly looked at me with fear in her eyes and asked, "What
are we going to do?"

"I'm not sure, but I'll think of something," I replied. I was
just as frightened as she was, but I did my best not to let it show.

I couldn't help but think back on my childhood. I lived in
more than thirty places, but one of my favorite places was a small
Midwest town. My friend across the street had goats. The boy
next door and I were friends, and his sister and I were a little sweet
on each other. But by the middle of my third year of grade school,
it all came to an end. Donnie had quit his job once again. He sold
my pony. We were evicted. My parents packed up the truck. I left
behind my friends and the best life I had ever known. We were
on our way across the state to stay with my aunt, my mother's
sister, and her husband, Donnie's brother. Yes, that's right. My
mother and her sister married brothers. At least they had indoor
plumbing. At that point, I didn't care about indoor plumbing. I
wanted my nice life back with my friends, my new bicycle, my
pony, and my cat. I couldn't stand the fact that it was all gone,
and I was angry.

Just thinking about my own children living anything close
to how I had grown up was nearly enough to make me sick.

Just face it! I thought to myself, and I did just that. First, I called the landowner. I dialed the phone and heard a man's voice ask, "Hello?"

I swallowed hard and said, "Hi, is this Stephen?"

"Yes," Stephen replied.

"This is Bill Richmond from your rental property," I said.

"Hi, Bill. I didn't expect to hear from you," he replied.

"I'm starting to feel a little bit better, and Shelly informed me that we are two months late on the rent."

"Yes, you are going to have to do something about that," he said in a firm voice. "I can't pay you all at once, but I can pay the current month plus some extra for what we are behind," I said in the most reassuring voice I could muster. "How much extra can you pay?" he asked. "I can pay an extra hundred dollars a month," I said. To my surprise, Stephen accepted the terms.

Next was the electric company, but they were not so friendly. The customer service person said, "We can set up a payment plan, but we need some money upfront." But I didn't have money. I called my friend Luis, who had brought the mattress set for the bed, to ask for help. He ran a nonprofit that helped low-income families with utility assistance. Luis agreed to pay the back payment that would allow me to set up the payment plan. Shelly was sitting in the bedroom because she didn't like to hear me deal with people. When I was finished, I went into the bedroom to give her the news.

She hugged my neck and said, "I knew you could do it!" I hugged her back, but I wasn't feeling the same excitement that she was. I saved my family from being evicted from our home, and I was able to keep the electricity on; however, I felt bad doing it.

The time came for the external fixators to be removed. The medical supply company picked up the hospital bed and the other equipment except for my electric wheelchair. That's when things began to decline again. I was starting to mix Valium with the pain pills. I lay in bed one night after a cocktail of pills, and I felt like my body was floating over the mattress. It wasn't an out-of-body experience, but it was enough to scare me. That was the breaking point for me.

I set the pills on my nightstand and stared them down for the next few days while I went through the withdrawal process. It started out with flu-like symptoms, but by the next day, it was like a serpent living deep in my soul, demanding to be fed! I sweated profusely. My stomach cramped, and I vomited until I was dehydrated. "Just take a couple. You will feel better!" Shelly pleaded.

"Why? So I can go through this all over again?" I snapped. My addiction to pain pills was short-lived, but it took a great deal of determination to become drug-free. My wife wasn't so fortunate. Try as she might, she couldn't quit.

Once the external fixators had been removed, I was now ready to be fitted for a prosthetic leg. First, we had to make a mold of my stump, and then people would have to build the lower part of the limb with prosthetic components, including a foot that looked somewhat real. The leg was completed much sooner than I expected, and Shelly drove me to pick it up. I wasn't sure what to expect, but I knew that I wanted to walk again!

Shelly and I waited patiently in an examination room with parallel bars stretching nearly the length of the room. "Are you ready for this?" Shelly asked.

"I think so," I replied.

Just then I heard a man's voice say, "How are you doing today, Bill?"

"Okay," I replied.

"Are you ready to walk?" the prosthetist asked as he stood there holding my leg.

"Sure!" I said with excitement in my voice. I took a seat in a chair at the end of the parallel bars.

After several attempts using a pull-sock, it was no use. This type of fit was not going to work. We settled on a dry powder, and my stump slid right into the socket. "Grab hold of the bars, and I will help you get up," he said. I stood on my feet for the first time in nearly a year. "How does it feel?" he asked.

"It feels great just to be on my feet, but I'm feeling a little nauseous," I replied. He gave me a moment to adjust to the new position, and he assured me this was normal.

"Okay, this is what I want you to do. Kick, plant, lock, kick, plant, lock, kick, plant, lock, kick, plant, lock," he said as he demonstrated how to use the prosthetic leg. "Kick your leg out, plant your heel, and then lock your knee. Are you ready?"

"Sure," I replied. *Kick, plant, lock,* I thought to myself as I walked from one end to the other end of the parallel bars. We would have to make a few adjustments, but on my next visit, I would use a walker and take the leg home.

A week passed quickly, and as promised, I received my new prosthetic leg. I was determined to walk from the car into the house, but I hated the thought of using the walker. It made me feel like an old person! I made it into the house, but I was exhausted. I sat on the sofa to relax. "Why don't you take your leg off and let me get you something to drink," Shelly said.

"I'll take a glass of ice water, but I'm going to leave the leg on," I replied.

After resting for a while, I was more determined than ever to walk without the walker. I navigated the walker to the hallway, so I could hold onto the wall on both sides. For the rest of the day, I walked back and forth, holding onto the walls for dear life. After a week or so of nearly wearing the paint off the walls, Shelly said, "Just let go and walk!"

No way! I thought to myself. However, eventually, I was able to go up and down the hallway using one hand. I could even go to the bathroom by myself. After continuing to practice in the hallway, Shelly said, "Let go with both hands!"

"I can't do it! I just can't!" I yelled. Shelly had a unique way of making me do things I really didn't want to.

One evening shortly after the kids went to bed, I started walking in the hallway, poking my head in each of their bedrooms and telling them good night. A while later, I heard Shelly's voice coming from our bedroom, "Bill, come in here." I walked to the door, going as far as I could while still holding onto the dresser. She was sitting on the edge of our bed with an emerald green nightgown on and her arms extended. "Come over here!" she said with a playful look on her face, which was something I had not seen in a very long time. I let go of the dresser and with my arms straight out to my sides for balance like I was walking a tightrope, I walked across the room and fell into Shelly's arms. We crashed onto the bed as she said, "I knew you could do it!" Shelly and I were intimate for the first time in a year.

It seemed like I went from a walker to a forearm crutch overnight. My confidence continued to build, and the paranoid thoughts I once had were finally gone. There was one last challenge I had to meet. *I can drive. I have a driver's license*, I thought to myself. I told Shelly about my idea of driving, but she wasn't as confident as I was.

"Are you sure you can drive with one leg?" she asked.

"I think so," I replied.

"At least let me go with you," she said.

I took the same approach as I did learning to walk. Shelly and I drove around the block until she couldn't stand it any longer. "You're doing really well. Maybe we can go a little farther tomorrow." In hardly no time at all, I was driving like a pro. I could drive Uncle Lenny to his doctor's appointments, take the kids to school, and do more for myself. Just when I thought that we were going to be okay, I was blindsided by some bad news from Stephen, our landlord. He informed me that he was going to sell the house and that we would have three months to move.

CHAPTER 5

Do not suppose that I have come to bring peace to
the earth. I did not come to bring peace but a sword.

—Matthew 10:34

SHORTLY AFTER WE received our income tax return, we found a house on the bank of a beautiful winding river in the eastern suburb of our city, but it needed some work. The roof needed coated with a sealant. The carport needed new shingles. The house needed to be painted both inside and out, and the yard was a mess. I offered to do the work, and in return, the rent would be adjusted to a price that we could afford.

Since I had just received my prosthetic leg, I was still struggling to walk, but with help from family and friends, I was confident we could complete the work in a timely manner. Shelly and a couple of her friends painted the inside, and some of the guys worked on the outside. The first weekend we accomplished quite a bit. The girls finished painting, and the guys completed the roof work and cut the grass. I was greatly appreciative of all of the work everyone was doing, but I felt worthless standing on the ground watching while everyone else did the work. Everyone agreed to come back the following weekend to finish up, but the next day I was determined to do some work on my own.

I set the ladder up on the side of the house, fixed up some paint, and slowly worked my way up the ladder. Just as I started to get myself into position, my leg fell off! There I was, standing on a ladder that was resting against the gable of the house. What a mess I had gotten myself into! Here I was at the top of the ladder, with a paintbrush in one hand and the paint bucket in the other. I had to think fast. *Now what am I going to do?* I asked myself as I looked down at my leg lying on the ground. I placed the paintbrush into the bucket and wrapped the wire bucket hanger around the rung of the ladder. I attempted to work my way down the ladder, using my arms and one leg. The bucket began to swing wildly! It was no use; I had to stop, or get a bucket of paint dumped on my head. I had no choice but to yell for Shelly. "Shelly, come quick. I need help!" I bellowed.

I heard her voice coming from the backyard. "Where are you?"

"Over here! I'm on the side of the house!" I yelled.

When she came around the corner of the house, she had a horrified look on her face. "What do you want me to do?" she yelled.

"Climb up the ladder behind me so I can hand you the bucket of paint," I said frantically. She climbed up and retrieved the bucket of paint, and when she was back on the ground, I started maneuvering my way down the ladder.

When I made it back to the ground and Shelly saw that all was well, she shook her head and said, "Are you crazy?" She didn't give me time to answer before she stomped back into the house.

As they promised, everyone showed up the next weekend to paint the exterior of the house. The work was finished. Everyone was gone, but once again, I couldn't help but feel worthless. *How will I ever be able to take care of my family?* I wondered. I found myself with my face buried into the back of the sofa, sobbing uncontrollably off and on for nearly a month. It hurt my wife to see me give up, so once again, she challenged me. The next time I was lying on the sofa, she asked, "Why don't you just get up and get a job?"

"Don't you think I want a job?" I asked her.

"Well, you're not going to find one lying there!" she rebuked. I was so angry that I called my wife some nasty choice words that I will not repeat, but the result was that I had a job the very next day!

A friend's father owned a printing company, and I went to work as sales representative. It was much different than the construction work that I was used to, but I was thrilled to find something that I could do. In fact, I could do it well! I earned "top sales person of the year," and I was invited to a dinner meeting where I was recognized and awarded a plaque for my office.

I had always been an entrepreneur at heart. Even as a child, I would find a way to earn some money whether I was raking leaves, mowing lawns, or shoveling snow. What comes to mind is the time when I was eight years old and really wanted a minibike.

We had converged on the home my aunt Pearl, who was Donnie's sister. Their family lived in a small rural community. Although I was about eight years old, I wasn't too young to notice the horrifying looks on Aunt Pearl and her husband's faces as we walked into their home. I can only imagine what they must have been thinking! I am sure it was something like, *Oh no! How long are they going to be here this time?* Their suspicions were correct. My parents were looking for a free place to stay once again. It was one of our longer stays, but certainly not our most pleasant one. I believe the intention was not to let my parents get too comfortable.

The children didn't offer to share their bedrooms, so the living room was where we slept for the next four months. My parents shared the sofa, Donnie's brother Lenny usually slept in the recliner, and Aunt Pearl made me a bed on the floor with blankets and a pillow. However, it wasn't all that bad. Donnie was doing odd jobs to earn some money, and I even got two ducks for Easter. The ducks were cute when they were little, but as they grew, they were becoming a real problem.

Donnie built a pen in the backyard for the ducks, but with the spring rain, the pen quickly became a mud pit. I knew our time to leave was coming near. My mother and my aunt were starting to make snarky comments to each other, and my uncle was tired of his backyard being used for a duck pen. My mother came out to talk to me about getting rid of the ducks about the same time the neighbor kid went racing by on his minibike. I didn't hear a word she said because I was mesmerized by the bike. After she asked me about three times if I would be interested in selling the ducks, I turned and said, "Sure, if I can get enough money to buy one of those!" I pointed to the minibike. She looked surprised because I think she was expecting more of a fight.

When Donnie saw that the coast was clear, he came over and announced that he might know someone who would buy the ducks. Donnie called his friend Charley, who had a pond, and asked him if he would be interested in the ducks. We borrowed a cage from the neighbor to transport the ducks in. I put them in the back of Donnie's old truck, and when we arrived at Charley's house, he was standing in the garage and waiting for us. I hoisted the duck cage out of the back of the truck and made my way up the driveway toward the garage. My mind raced with thoughts. *I wonder how much he will pay me for the ducks.* As I continued to go over my sales strategy, I heard Charley say, "Hi, Billy, those are some good-looking ducks you have."

"They are great ducks," I replied. I walked into the garage with my game face on, ready for an old-fashioned duck-trading throw down. That all changed when Donnie nudged me and pointed to the other side of the garage. I turned my head in the direction he was pointing, and I couldn't believe my eyes. In the corner of the garage was a minibike! My eyes locked onto the bike, and once again I didn't hear a word anyone said.

I quickly turned to Charley and asked, "Can I ride the minibike?"

"You'd better ask your parents first," he replied.

My mother and Donnie smiled and gave a nod to go ahead. It wasn't as fancy as the neighbor boy's bike. In fact, it wasn't much more than a small frame, two wheels, and a small engine, but I didn't care. When Charley pulled the rope and the bike started, I was the happiest little boy in town. I straddled the bike, and Charley pointed to the pond and said, "You can ride around the pond, but just be careful!"

"I will!" I shouted.

My mom, Donnie, and Charley watched me as I carefully made my way around the pond. As soon as the adults went back into the garage and were out of sight, I started going faster and faster, and before long, I was going as fast as the bike would go. It was even more fun than I expected, but the fun came to an end when I noticed Donnie motioning for me to come back to the garage. I held up one finger to signal one more lap as I raced by. I made my way back to the garage with a big smile on my face. As I got off the bike, I thanked Charley and said, "That was really fun. Do you want to sell it?"

"Well, I got it for my kids when they were younger, but they don't ride it anymore," he replied. "How much money do you have?"

I quickly pulled a bread bag out of my pocket, which contained my life savings of four dollars. "I have two ducks and four bucks!" I exclaimed.

"Well, Billy, I think you are getting the best end of the deal, but I really want those ducks. So you have yourself a minibike."

"Really?" I shouted. "It's really mine?"

"Yes, it's really yours. As long as it's okay with your parents," Charley replied.

"Thank you! Thank you!" I shouted in almost a state of disbelief. "Can I ride around the pond a few more times?" I asked. As the adults were standing around and drinking beer, I rode the minibike around the pond as fast as it would go until it ran out of gas. I pushed the bike back to the garage, and Donnie put it in the back of the truck. I thanked Charley again, and we were on our way back to Aunt Pearl's house without the ducks but with a minibike that would keep me occupied for about the next week.

A week or so later, the inevitable happened. Donnie and his sister got into a huge argument, and we were headed south. My mother was quick to tell me that it didn't snow where we were going. The first thought that came to my mind was that I could ride my minibike all year. Just like they promised, after traveling for a few days, we arrived and moved in with a friend of my parents. She was a single mother with three children, two boys and a girl. It wasn't all bad. I shared a room with the youngest boy who was the same age as I was. I even had a bed, blankets, and a pillow!

Behind the house there was an alley that was mostly sand, and I raced from one end to the other with my minibike. However, the fun was short-lived. The police showed up and said that I couldn't ride the minibike in the alley anymore. Donnie was quick to say that since there wasn't anywhere to ride the minibike, we might as well sell it. I really wanted to keep the bike, but I knew there wasn't any use in arguing. The bike was going to be sold, and I wouldn't see any money for it. I shrugged my shoulders and said, "May as well." I was almost nine years old by this time, but even at such a young age, I learned not to count on anything for the long term. Without knowing it, I was becoming conditioned to live for the moment and enjoy the present because it probably wouldn't last.

After receiving my sales award, I continued working as a salesperson for the printing company, and I began to find my worth in my job. I even started doing little things around the house, but I wasn't prepared for my next project. I was getting increasingly sure of myself as every day passed, and I began to believe that I could tackle the bank that lead to the river.

With a prosthetic leg on my right side and a forearm crutch on my left side, I rounded up a machete and a couple of saws from the garage. My son, Andy, who was thirteen at the time, and I began to take on the overgrown bank. After a little while, it was apparent that we had very little success. I was weak from a recent yearlong stay in a wheelchair. I only had my prosthetic leg for about three months, and my balance was not very good. But I refused to let my son watch me give up, so I pressed forward. I was unprepared but grateful for what happened next.

As we were taking a break to get something to drink, I noticed a giant of a man and two young boys walking through the yard. I approached the man and asked if I could help him. The man said, "Hi! I'm your neighbor from across the street. Why don't you let us do this for you?"

I said, "Thank you. I can't afford to pay anyone, so my son and I were going to do it ourselves."

The man smiled and said, "We don't want any money. We just thought you could use some help. My name is Ryan, and these are my sons, James and Jason." I extended my hand for a handshake, introduced my son, Andy, and myself. Ryan said, "If you will pick a few lemons off your tree and make a pitcher of lemonade, we'll get started." I thanked Ryan and walked toward the tree, somewhat confused, wondering why someone would do this for me.

I picked six large lemons and went into the house to make the lemonade. Still confused about my encounter, I told my wife what had happened. She peeked out of the window facing the canal and said, "Are those the people who live across the street with the basketball hoop at the end of their driveway?"

"Yes. They seem like very nice people," I replied. I returned to the backyard with a pitcher of lemonade and five glasses of ice. The friendships that began developing that day were nothing short of amazing!

After they drank the lemonade, Ryan told me that I could take it easy and that he and the boys would have this done in no time. I gladly accepted Ryan's offer and took a seat on the dock.

What I observed was magical. Ryan and the boys cut the trees down, cut them into the proper length for recycling, tied them, and dragged them to the curb without one complaint. To watch Ryan interact with the boys was also amazing. He let them be boys and fool around, but he didn't let them go too far. As I continued to watch Ryan, I noticed that there was something different about him. He was just so happy and so full of joy. I pondered, *How can anyone be so happy? He must have a great job. They live in a very nice home. How can I be as happy as my new friend, Ryan?*

After the work was done, Ryan said, "We're going home to get cleaned up and get some ice cream. Would you and Andy like to join us?" Before long, Ryan pulled into my driveway, and Andy and I climbed into his van.

At first, I made small talk, but Ryan got right down to business. He asked me if we attended a church. I replied, "No, my family and I have never gone to church." I went on to say that even growing up, I could not remember going to church.

Ryan exclaimed, "Well, you don't know what you're missing. The boys and I go on Wednesday night for Bible study and then play basketball afterward, and on Sunday, we go to services. It's really a nice church."

"It sounds like it," I replied.

"So what do you think?" Ryan asked, "Will you and Andy be joining us?"

"I don't know," I said with some hesitation in my voice.

Just then Andy piped up from the back seat and said, "Come on, Dad. It sounds like fun."

"I don't know." I said. "I promised your sister I would do something with her on Wednesday." Ryan asked me if I was talking about the little blonde girl. "Yes," I replied, "that is my youngest. Her name is Denise."

Ryan said, "You are welcome to bring her too if you would like."

Again, I hesitated and said I would think about it. Once

again, Andy piped up from the back seat and said, "Dad, if you don't want to go, can I go with the boys? I really want to go. It sounds like fun!"

I said, "I don't mind, but you'd better ask Mr. Jackson."

Ron replied, "Oh, absolutely, and you can bring your little sister too." Andy was excited about going but not about bringing his little sister.

Just as the boys were eating the last few bites of their ice cream, Ryan asked me if I had time to go over and look at the church. I said, "Sure. Why not?" We all piled back into the van, and before long, he pulled into a huge parking lot with a big modern building off to the right.

Ryan said, "Here it is. Let me give you a tour." He drove through a gate and said, "This is a fishing pond, and over there in the field is where we camp out sometimes." As we drove out of the gate, Ryan was talking about the gym, the music room, and the many classes they had for people of all ages. James spotted some kids he knew from church and asked his dad if they could get out and talk to them. The three boys piled out of the van to visit with the other boys and that gave Ryan an opportunity to talk without any distractions.

I complimented Ryan on what nice boys he had, and he said, "It isn't anything I did. The glory goes to God."

Ryan stumped me with his reply, but almost immediately, I commented, "But you seem like such a happy and content person."

"That's because I have someone much greater than myself to depend on." By this time, I was really confused, but he quickly noticed my confusion and said, "Our Lord and Savior, Jesus Christ."

"Oh," I replied, but then I became very quiet because I didn't know much about religion.

Ryan said, "I don't want to pressure you, but do you know where you are going if you were to die, or for that matter, do you know where your children would go? That's something you might want to think about."

I thought for a moment. *Where will I go if I die today? Will I ever see my children or my family and friends again?* I had more questions than answers. He quickly noticed the puzzled look on my face and said, "If you have any questions, I would be glad to answer them, and if I can't, I will get someone who can."

I said, "I'm sure I will have some questions."

Ryan replied, "When I have questions, I pray about it, and then I go to scripture because I am sure the answers are there. The Lord will usually reveal them to me, but if I'm still struggling, I ask someone who knows the Bible better than I do, such as an elder at my church or the pastor."

"That's incredible to have such a network of people that help one another." Ryan just smiled.

Before long, the boys were climbing back into the van, and we were on the five-mile ride home. We pulled into the driveway, and everyone said their goodbyes. Ryan said to me, "I hope that you, Andy, and Denise can go to church with us on Wednesday."

I replied, "Yeah, I hope so too." I walked into the house, replaying our conversation over and over in my head, but the thing that kept coming back to me was where I would go if I died today.

Just as we came through the dining room, Shelly met us and asked, "Did you have fun?"

"Yes, it was a good time," I replied, but then we got into a discussion about religion.

She said, "What do you know about religion?"

"Well, I know there's a heaven and a hell, and I know that Jesus died on the cross to pay for our sins. Let me ask you a question. Do you know where you would go if you died today?"

She replied sarcastically, "Does it matter if I am dead?"

"Yeah, I think it does," I replied. The conversation with my wife wasn't going anywhere, so I decided to go to church with Ryan and the children on Wednesday and ask my questions.

Ryan pulled into the driveway about 6:30 on Wednesday evening, and Denise, Andy, and I climbed into the van. Ryan said, "I'm glad everyone could make it."

"I am as well, but I do have some questions," I said.

He smiled and said, "I will do my best to answer them." In just a few minutes, we were at the church. After Bible study, the children went to the gym, and Ryan suggested that he and I sit in comfortable chairs just outside of the gym where we could hear each other better. He said, "So, what are your questions?"

"Well, how do I know where I will go if I die, or how do I know where my family members will go?"

Ryan said, "Let's go to scripture and see what the Bible tells us."

By the time he finished, my head was spinning! I believed the Bible to be the absolute truth, but I still had so many questions. Andy, Denise, and I continued to go to church with Ryan and his children. I tried to get Nancy to come with us, and she begrudgingly went once in a while; however, Shelly refused to have any part of it. I was perplexed why my wife refused to go to church and learn about Jesus, who died on the cross to pay for our sins. The more I tried to drag my wife to church, the more she resisted. My family was self-destructing, and I felt helpless. Nancy was starting to experiment with drugs, and Shelly was addicted to opiates. I was not blameless. I drank sometimes until I would black out. However, it terrified me that Nancy was beginning to use drugs. All I could think about was my own childhood when drugs nearly destroyed me.

By the time I was seventeen years old, I was homeless and taking shelter at a drug house. I was working six days a week and still wasn't making enough to support my habit. Shortly after I moved into the drug house, my job ended for the summer, and I turned to selling drugs fulltime.

One afternoon after selling all that I had, I was walking back to the house to pick up more drugs, and police cars began to pass me. City cops, the state highway patrol, the sheriff's department, and even DEA vans were all zooming past me. As I got closer, I realized they were going to the house I was staying at. Sure enough, it was a raid, and they took everyone in the house to jail. I panicked and turned to walk away as fast as I could without being obvious. I held my head down and didn't look at anyone. *Are they looking for me too? Am I going to jail?* I wondered. I was terrified and all alone. After getting what I believed to be a safe distance from the house, I cut between an arcade and a hamburger stand to go to the beach. I sat on the shore of Lake Erie, looking over to where I thought Canada might be, wondering if I would be safe there. The last bit of meth that I did earlier was wearing off, and the last thing I remember was lying back for a minute to clear my head.

Suddenly, I felt someone's foot nudge me and heard a man's voice ask, "Are you all right?"

I sat up and said, "I'm just waiting for someone. I must have fallen asleep. What time is it?"

"It's 6:10," the man replied. I didn't tell the man that I had been sleeping there all night. I rose to my feet and stumbled up the hill to the strip. The strip is a half-mile section with bars, restaurants, and arcades that lined both sides of the street. I had less than $100 in my pocket from the sales of the drugs the day before. I was sure that the place I was staying at was no longer available. It felt like I didn't have a friend left or anyone to depend on.

I lived through the worst time of my young life, but my fear was that Nancy might not. I don't believe my new friend and mentor, Ryan, knew what a mess my family was in, but he continued to lead by example and tell me about scripture.

Before long, Denise, Andy, and I were all going to church with Ryan, James, and Jason every Sunday and sometimes on Wednesday night. It didn't take long to see that the life I was living was not honoring God. We continued to go to church every Sunday. Andy joined the youth group, and Denise attended AWANA, a Bible-based program for children. I was so proud of Denise when she came home from church and told me that she had memorized her first Bible verse, John 3:16. I asked her to recite it for me just as her brother was walking up the driveway. "Come over here, Andy!" she screeched, grinning from ear to ear, displaying her missing two front teeth. I memorized John 3:16, and I want you to hear it! Andy walked over to join us, and Denise began, "For God so loved the world that he gave his one and only Son, that whosoever believes in him shall not perish but have eternal life." I looked at Andy and raised my eyebrows, with a surprised look on my face.

Andy returned the surprised look and said, "I think that's right!"

"It is!" Denise rejoiced. "I learned it in church today!" I hugged my seven-year-old daughter's neck and kissed her cheek with a tear in my eye because I was so proud of her.

Andy rubbed his little sister's head and said, "That's great!" Andy and I stood there with a stunned look on our faces.

Neither of us wanted to break the awkward silence, but we both knew what the other one was thinking. I broke the silence first and remarked, "I've never learned any Bible verses in my life."

"Me either," he replied.

"I think it's time to start reading the Bible when a seven-year-old is reciting scripture to us!" I exclaimed.

"I guess so," Andy said and chuckled as he was leaving to play basketball.

Johnny, who was one of the boys in the neighborhood and who was also about Denise's age, came riding up on his Harley-Davidson bicycle and asked her to ride with him. Denise wasn't moving fast enough to suit him, so he put his hands on his hips and asked, "Are you coming or not?" I believe Johnny was a little sweet on Denise, but she was oblivious. I didn't have to worry too much. They were only seven years old. I couldn't help but think about my first girlfriend when I was about their same age.

Just before I began first grade, my parents pooled all of their resources together, and we were able to move to our own apartment on Main Street. I was sure this time it would be different. We lived right across the street from a candy store. The next day before school started, my mother gave me lunch money and an extra nickel to buy some penny candy at the little store as long as I promised not to eat it in class. I looked out the window and saw kids going in and out of the store, carrying their little brown bags full of candy.

So when it was time to leave, the crowd at the candy store had thinned out, and I walked across the street and laid my nickel on the counter. I picked out as many root beer barrels as a nickel would buy and said, "Thank you. My name is Billy. I will be back again. I live right across the street."

That is when I heard the voice of an angel say, "Hi, my name is Diane. I live upstairs. Are you going to school?" I told her I was on my way to school now, and she said, "You are a little early, but I will walk with you if you would like."

I smiled and said, "Sure!"

Diane and I left the candy store and began our short journey to the school. Just a few minutes into our walk, Diane looked over and said, "Would you like to hold my hand?" My palms got sweaty, and my mind raced with thoughts. *She is the most beautiful person I had ever laid my eyes on, and her parents own a candy store. I will probably have free candy forever!* I reached over and clutched her hand. I was far too young to understand the intricate details about boyfriend and girlfriend, but there was something about this I really liked. I felt like I could do anything. This was the best place I had ever lived and the best school I had ever gone to. Some children would comment about my thick glasses and my birdlike appearance, but it did not take long for me to figure out that if I acted like a clown, children would laugh at what I was doing instead of what I looked like.

Diane and I barely had a two-week courtship. We walked to school every day holding hands, and life could not be better— that is, until I was clowning around at the lunch table one day. I squirted ketchup into a bowl of tartar sauce. Most of the children laughed, but someone told the lunch attendant. The attendant approached our table and said, "Who did that?" In a panic, I pointed to the person who was seated on the left side of me, and that was Diane.

She shrieked, "I didn't do that! You did!" The other children confirmed what she said, and I was sent to the principal's office and lost my girlfriend at the same time!

For the next several days, the Bible verse that Denise had learned, John 3:16, consumed me. *Jesus really died for my sins*, I thought to myself. I wanted to know more about God's Word and more about Jesus.

After church on Sunday, as we were waiting for the children to come out of their classes, I told Ryan about my desire to learn more about God. "Keep coming to church and reading the Bible," he said. I didn't mind going to church, but the thought of reading the Bible terrified me. I had a third- to fifth-grade reading level at best, and the Bible just seemed too difficult for me to handle. I knew I would have to read it, but I didn't have any idea how I would accomplish it. I was too embarrassed to share my thoughts with Ryan, and Satan tried to convince me that Ryan would believe that I was stupid. I listened to Satan's lies for a while. There was some sort of spiritual warfare going on in my head, but I was clueless. I was sure Ryan would understand, but then Satan would raise his ugly head again and penetrate my mind with his lies. Ryan was a very smart guy with a great job. *How can he possibly understand that I am thirty-five years old and can't read?* I thought to myself.

A few weeks later, Ryan asked, "So how are you doing with the Bible reading?"

It was the moment of truth. *What do I do?* I wondered. *Make up some ridiculous lie that he probably wouldn't believe or just tell him?* I hung my head in shame and embarrassment and simply said, "I can't read well enough to study the Bible."

Without thinking twice, he said, "I have the Bible on audio tapes if you would like to borrow them."

"Yes. That would be great!" I exclaimed. That was the first time that I had ever told anyone about my reading problem, and it wasn't as bad as I thought. If I would have believed Satan's lies and chosen to be dishonest, I am sure my life would have had a much different outcome.

I listened to the tapes in the car, usually when the kids and I were going somewhere, but now and then I would try to get Shelly to listen to a few Bible verses. She didn't respond well to my forceful tactics. She would give me a dirty look and ask "Can you put the radio on instead?"

"Will you just listen for a few minutes?" I asked.

"I want to hear some music!" she said. "I already know what the Bible says. I've read it."

"Well do you believe it?"

"Of course, I believe it!" she exclaimed. "But religion is a personal thing, and I am just not ready." Shelly pushed the button to eject the tape, and then she turned the volume up on the radio. To her surprise, a Christian song came blasting through the speakers!

I chuckled and asked her, "Do you believe in coincidence?"

"Very funny!" she snapped as she turned the radio dial to a popular classic rock station.

"Please turn the radio down for a minute," I asked her. Reluctantly, she did, and I said, "I don't mean to be so pushy, but I just want what is best for our family."

"How do you know what is best?" she asked.

"I know what we are doing is not the best we can do." I replied. The argument wasn't gaining any positive results, so I ended the topic of religion, and Shelly turned the radio back up a few notches.

Andy, Denise, and I continued to go to church with Ryan and his two sons, but my family became more divided. Shelly barricaded herself in the bedroom almost every evening. I was sure she spent a great deal of time smoking marijuana. The tipping point was when a neighbor came over to greet me as I returned home from church. He said, "I walked through your side yard to get down to the canal, and I smelled marijuana coming from your house."

"Are you sure the smell was coming from my house?" I asked.

He assured me that it was. I stormed into the house, both embarrassed and angry. I wasn't surprised by what I found. Shelly was as happy as could be. The house reeked with pot smoke! "I am sick of this nonsense!" I bellowed. "If you give Andy or Denise any of that crap, I will have you put in jail!" I screamed. Andy and Denise were with Ryan and the boys, so I went out to sit on the dock for some quiet time. I held my head in my hands and asked myself, "How could my wife be acting this way?" It was almost as if a coconut fell out of one of the big trees that hung over the dock and hit me on top of the head! The answer was simple. It was my own fault. I had tolerated Shelly's drug abuse for our entire marriage. In fact, I had even participated at first. I didn't feel like I had any choice but to go to Ryan with my dilemma.

I asked Ryan for help, but at the same time, I skirted the issue and tried to downplay it. His initial answer was the same every time. "Let's pray about it!" he said. After we prayed, Ryan said, "You may have some difficult choices to make, but I wouldn't recommend trying it on your own."

I tried to reason with Shelly, but she rebutted by saying she had smoked pot since she was a teenager and she wasn't going to stop now. I prayed daily and tried to talk to Shelly without being too judgmental, but she wasn't having any of it. It was more apparent than ever. Ryan was right. I couldn't do it on my own!

The following week at church, the pastor announced that they were going to be having a baptism service in a couple of weeks. My son, Andy, and I were baptized the same day in front of the congregation. I'm not sure what I expected or if I even understood salvation. I could only hope that things would get better; however, things got much worse.

Nancy was becoming unruly, and Shelly was more combative than ever. Our house was divided—Shelly and Nancy on one side and Andy, Denise, and me on the other. Shelly and I couldn't even look at each other without making a sarcastic remark, which usually turned into an all-out screaming match. A short time later, Shelly got a job at a local retail store that made it possible for her to afford her drug habit.

Once again, a few months later, the person who owned the house we were living in informed me that he had sold the house and that we would have to move again.

CHAPTER 6

For the love of money is a root of all kinds of evil.
Some people, eager for money, have wandered from
the faith and pierced themselves with many griefs.

—1 Timothy 6:10

W E FOUND A house in the same neighborhood, but it was a
lot more expensive. With Shelly's income from the store,
my income from disability, and what I was able to earn, we were
doing okay financially. We bought a computer and game system
for the kids as well as an above-ground pool that the family could
enjoy in the backyard. The kids would invite other children
from the neighborhood over to swim in the pool. I would grill
hot dogs, and Shelly always served the children drinks. I felt so
grateful and thanked God for the nice things that my family had.

Ryan was still driving Denise, Andy, and me to church every
Sunday. I felt the love of God, but the division of my family was
gnawing at me like cancer. *There must be a way to get Shelly and
Nancy to come to church with us*, I thought to myself. I prayed, "Lord,
I am not asking for much. I just want a family that will serve you.
I pray, Father, that Shelly will quit using drugs and that she and
Nancy will start coming to church with us. It is in Jesus's name
that I pray!"

However, things continued to get worse, but I continued to pray. When Nancy was sixteen, Shelly allowed her to drop out of school. Nancy was regularly taking the car while we were sleeping, and her drug habit was much worse than I realized. I prayed earnestly, but it seemed liked the Lord didn't hear my prayers. I asked myself, "Have I messed things up so bad that the Lord isn't going to fix my family?"

Nancy continued to take the car while we were sleeping, but I eventually caught her in the act. I woke up in the middle of the night and checked the driveway. Sure enough, the car was gone, and so was Nancy. I was furious! She didn't have a driver's license. She wasn't insured, and she had very little experience driving. I took my belt off, sat in the dark living room, and waited for her to come home. My fear that she would get hurt or hurt someone else quickly subsided, and anger overcame me as I saw the car's headlights shining in the window. Nancy looked like she had seen a ghost when she came into the house and saw me standing there with a belt in my hand! However, I just couldn't do it. I was too angry! I held my hand out, demanding the keys. "Go to bed. We'll deal with this tomorrow," I said in a surprisingly calm voice. I put the keys in my pocket and laid the belt on the sofa. Tears welled up in my eyes as I asked myself, "Would I be just like him?" referring to my adopted father, Donnie.

A short time later, I met a real estate agent that said he could help me buy a house for what I was paying in rent. With some creative financing and stretching the truth a bit, we owned a home within two months. The payments were a couple of hundred dollars more per month than we anticipated, and the utilities were almost double. However, it didn't matter. We would make it somehow. I was sure that my family would be much happier if we owned our own home.

I was wrong again, and within six months we were in over our heads. First, the electric was shut off. No sooner than I got the electric restored, the water was shut off, and before long the city quit picking up the garbage. Even with Shelly's income and my social security disability income, it still wasn't enough money. The children and I weren't going to church with Ryan and his children anymore. I took my eyes off of the Lord, and Satan set up shop. As much as I hated it, I felt defeated. Satan was having his way with my family and me.

Andy and I started hanging out at the local pool hall. Andy was seventeen by this time. In a fit of rage, Shelley said, "Why don't you just buy a bar?"

Sarcastically, I exclaimed, "That's not a bad idea!" Andy overheard the argument and informed me that there was a lounge that was vacant in the strip mall at the corner. Out of curiosity, we went there and began peeking in the windows. Curiosity quickly turned into interest when the property manager approached us. After a brief conversation with him, I found out that the place could be bought for almost nothing. Before long, I met with the person that was paying the lease. He owned a vending company, and he was more interested in vending than he was in the lounge. "It had to be more lucrative than what I was doing, and it was actually legal!" I told myself. He agreed to pay three months of the lease while I secured the necessary licenses and got the place ready to open—that is, as long as I would agree to keep his vending machines and split the profit.

I told him that I would let him know the next day because I wanted to talk it over with my wife. "Just let me know," he said.

"Let me be clear," I said. "I am required to give you half of the take from the vending machines. You do the repairs, and the rest of the business is mine, right?"

"That's right!" he replied. "I will have my lawyer fix up the necessary papers and have the property manager put the lease in your name if you choose to go ahead with this venture."

I went home that evening and told Shelley that I did as she instructed. "I bought a bar!" I yelled.

She looked at me with a bit of disbelief and said, "How did you do that without any money?"

"Well, it's not official yet, but the owner offered me a deal," I replied.

I told her about the offer, and she said sarcastically, "If you can pull this off, remind me to tell you to buy a diamond mine in South Africa!"

The following day I checked the availability of the license to sell beer and wine. I was confident that I could obtain the license, so I took the deal. I thought that it would be a nice place for people to have a couple of beers, but I knew I was lying to myself. However, I had to justify my decision to be a bar owner.

The place was open in thirty days. I had never owned a bar before, but I visited plenty of them. I was sure I would be successful, but I didn't have any idea how demanding it would be. Before it was over, I was working 105 hours a week. I didn't have any time to spend with my family. Out of guilt, I hired a nanny for my youngest daughter, Denise. Denise and the nanny had great fun! They went to the movies every weekend, ate at restaurants, and did anything else Denise wanted to do. I managed to squeeze out enough time twice a month to go with Denise so she could get her nails done. She was twelve years old, and she had sculptured nails, a cell phone, and a nanny, but that didn't stop the bar business from devouring me like a roaring lion.

I was growing weaker by the day. The long hours were taking a toll on me. I had a full staff, but it seemed like every time I left, something bad happened. Employees were stealing from me. Customers were not being taken care of properly, and anything that could go wrong did unless I was there to babysit them. On a rare occasion, I went home for dinner. However, there was one particular night that I would not soon forget.

After returning to the bar from dinner with my family, I was furious at what I found. A man tipped his head back to take a drink of his beer, and being drunk, he fell off the barstool right at my feet! I helped the man up and made sure that he was not hurt. One of my regular customers gave him a ride home. I reprimanded the bartender and assured her if that ever happened again, she wouldn't have a job. That blew a hole in my earlier idea that people would only have a couple of beers and go home! I was certain that I had to be there from opening to closing seven days a week.

I knew this was all wrong, and from time to time, I would think about when the kids and I went to church with Ryan and his children. However, for whatever reason, I couldn't resist the temptation of local gang members hanging around the bar and the money that came with them. In what seemed like no time at all, my bar was packed wall to wall every night! All I had to do was turn my head while the local gang members and drug dealers conducted their business. I was making more money than ever, and I was getting all the free cocaine I could possibly take. The music was blasting out of the speakers from the live band, and there wasn't an empty seat in the place.

One night I was standing out front, gazing in the window. I was as high as could be on cocaine. My eyes were bulging, and I was quenching my thirst with a beer when I heard a car blowing its horn. I looked over my shoulder and couldn't have been more surprised when Ryan motioned for me to come over to talk to him. I set the beer on the windowsill and slowly started to approach the car. All I could think about was that this was the man who had led me to Christ. I could only imagine how Adam must have felt when he was hiding in the garden of Eden and God called his name.

Ryan, being a humble man, didn't try to chastise me, but he did say, "I don't think you are going to be passing many tracts out in there!"

"No, probably not," I replied. I was incredibly embarrassed, but Ryan and I had a nice conversation. After a short while, he drove away, and I went back inside the bar. Ryan was right. I wasn't passing out any tracts in the bar or anywhere else for that matter. Once again, with just a few words, he planted a seed. I knew my friend was right, but I was not ready to give it up. The Cadillac, plenty of money, and the nanny for my daughter would all be gone if I did.

A couple months later, I went to Ryan with a troubling question. I asked him, "Why do people who are doing things that they aren't supposed to be doing get rewarded?"

"Do you mean bar owners and drug dealers?" he asked.

I nodded my head and said, "Yes, I guess I do."

Ryan, who had great wisdom and wasn't someone to mince words, knew just what I needed. As usual, he gave it to me straight when he said, "Satan gives gifts too. You should take a look at 1 Timothy 6:10." Eventually, I opened my Bible to 1 Timothy. There it was as plain as day! It read, "For the love of money is the root of all kinds of evil." I surely couldn't argue with the Bible!

A month later the property owner of the strip mall where the bar was located at informed me that he had a nice house for sale. He sure wasn't kidding. The home was in a housing development in a decent area, and it had a screened-in pool! Just as I was pondering how I could afford the house, one of my regular customers asked if I would be interested in selling the bar. He made a generous offer, and within thirty days, the bar was sold. After that, we purchased the house with a pool. Now I was sure that I was going to be able to give my family the life they deserved.

We moved into the new home, opened the pool, landscaped the yard, and painted the outside of the house. Before long, my children made friends with the kids in the neighborhood, and they were all swimming in the pool while I would grill hot dogs for them on the pool deck. I got a job at a large retail store across town and bought Shelly a late-model sports car. On the outside it appeared that we were living the American dream. What I failed to notice while working at the bar and being absent from home was that my wife's drug habit had become even worse. When I left the bar, I immediately stopped doing cocaine, and I expected my wife to stop her drug habit as well. However, it wasn't to be. In fact, I don't believe she could have stopped immediately even if she wanted to. Our home, once again, became divided, and even worse than the last time. This time, however, I wasn't asking the Lord for any direction. I was certain I could pull my family together on my own. I couldn't have been more wrong!

Andy joined the military, and Shelly and I continued to have marital problems. I tried everything I could to avoid a divorce, but of course, I wasn't depending on anyone greater than myself. More than ever, what I needed was guidance from the Lord, but I still thought I could do it on my own. I gave my wife an ultimatum. "You have two weeks to make a choice. It's either drugs or your family!" I shouted at her one evening.

"You know I want my family, but I have had addiction problems since before we were married," she said, sobbing.

"I know! I am not asking you to quit in two weeks; however, I'm just asking you to start moving in that direction. Just call some treatment programs to see what's available."

I checked with her over the next week and a half to see if she had done as I had asked. She hadn't, and the time I dreaded was coming near. I made arrangements with Jack, who was our neighbor, to drive Denise and me from Florida to Ohio. He agreed for a fair price. On the morning of the fourteenth day, I asked Shelly again what her decision was. She informed me that she couldn't do it right now. We both agreed that I would be able to take better care of Denise, so Shelly didn't fight me when I said that I was going to take Denise with me up north to be with my family. Shelly's only requests were that we wait until she went to work before we packed and that I didn't take her car.

I respected both wishes, and before she returned home from work, we were gone. I took two brown paper bags with some clothes, and Denise packed her things in as many suitcases as she could get her hands on! We climbed into Jack's little blue truck for the twelve-hundred-mile journey back home. It was not a comfortable ride, to say the least. The truck was only meant for the driver and one passenger; however, with some pillows between the bucket seats, we altered it for a driver and two passengers. I was sure I was doing the right thing, but that didn't stop me from weeping as I watched the skyline of the city disappear from the side mirror. I wasn't sure what our life back home would be like, but I was sure it would be much different than when I had left.

CHAPTER 7

You are the light of the world. A city on a hill
cannot be hidden. Neither do people light a
lamp and put it under a bowl. Instead they put
it on its stand, and it gives light to everyone
in the house. In the same way, let your light
shine before men, that they may see your good
deeds and praise your Father in heaven.

—Matthew 5:14–16

M Y MOTHER AND her boyfriend, Fred, invited Denise and
I to stay with them, but the welcome didn't last long.
The first couple of days were difficult, but I mustered up the
courage, swallowed my pride, and applied for public assistance,
including food assistance and cash benefits. Then I went to the
social security office and applied for disability benefits.

Denise had never seen snow before, and she was very excited!
It was mid-November. The snow was hanging off the tree
branches with a light dusting on the ground. It looked almost
magical outside. Even better than that was what the mailman
had left in the mailbox. We received the food assistance, cash
benefits, and even a medical card so that we could go to the
doctor. It wasn't much, but it seemed that things were looking
up. I wasn't sure how to feel about the public assistance money,

but I knew I needed every penny of it and more just to take care of my daughter's basic needs.

Dan, an old friend from childhood, stopped over to visit one day just as the phone rang. Mom answered it, but the person on the other end was very brief. Mom hung up the phone and began to cry. "What's wrong?" I asked.

"It was Fred, and he's drunk. He said that he won't come back until you and Denise are gone. I don't know what to do. Even with both of our incomes, we can't keep up with the bills!" she said. I didn't know how much money it would take to cover the bills, but I don't believe it would have mattered anyway. The bottom line was that we had to leave so Fred would come back.

Dan reluctantly said, "You and Denise can stay with me for a while."

"It looks like we might have to," I replied. A short time after he made the offer, we had his car packed with our things.

Denise shared a room with Dan's daughter, who was only there on the weekends, and I slept on a roll-a-way bed in the living room. It seemed like a decent temporary arrangement. Denise and I did all of the cooking and cleaning. I bought all of the food and helped with the utility bills. However, this arrangement wouldn't last. Dan woke up one Saturday morning and said, "This is my home, and I am tired of sharing it!" I called my sister, Cindy, to see if we could stay with her and her family. My sister and her husband are very kind people, but I'm sure they weren't looking forward to taking in two more family members. My sister informed me that I would have to come over and talk to her husband, Brian.

Dan dropped us off at Cindy and Brian's home. My brother-in-law and I went to the basement to talk. I was at the end of my rope and felt like I was going to have a complete breakdown. I tried to fight back the tears, but it was no use. The tears were flowing. I wiped my eyes and told him that we didn't have anywhere to go, that Denise and I were homeless. He asked how long we would be staying. I hung my head and said, "I don't know."

"Don't worry about it. You and Denise can stay here for as long as you need to," he said. I thanked him with tears in my eyes. I walked over and sat on the bottom step. I'm sure Brian could sense that I wanted to be alone, so he returned to the main floor. I held my head in my hands and sobbed. *I'm going to raise my daughter just like I was raised*, I thought to myself. It didn't occur to me to pray. I dried my eyes on the sleeve of my shirt and went upstairs to find my sister making lunch. Brian sat at one end of the table, and he asked me to sit at the other end. Cindy and Lindsey, the eldest daughter, sat on one side, and Amy, the youngest daughter, and Denise sat on the other side. I was amazed at how smooth everything went and how no one had a harsh word to say. I started reflecting back on childhood and couldn't remember ever having a more peaceful meal.

We lived with my sister and her family for the next several months. It was one of the most positive experiences of my life, and I hoped that one day I could have a family like this. It amazed me how my sister's family functioned. Everyone had a job. Brian came home from work first, so he made dinner, and afterward, the girls cleaned the table and did the dishes. I think what amazed me the most was when I asked what I should do with my dirty clothes. Lindsey instructed me to throw them at the bottom of the basement stairs and the next day they appeared back in the closet, clean and fresh. She did a load of laundry almost every day.

My sister and her family had a new home with modern appliances. I'm not sure what I liked better—the pool table or the double-door refrigerator with an ice and water dispenser! At any rate, it was the nicest house that I had ever lived in. Although the house was wonderful, what I really appreciated the most was getting to know my sister and her family. I formed a new appreciation for what good and decent people they were and how they raised their children with the same values. And then the moment I had been waiting for finally came. I received a phone call that confirmed that I was approved for social security disability. The money, including a retroactive payment, was placed into a bank account for Denise and me.

We moved to a small apartment complex on the edge of town that accepted the government subsidies I qualified for. The apartment was just half of the battle. We didn't have any furniture, not a blanket, a pot, a pan, or anything else to furnish an apartment. With the back payment money from social security, I was able to buy new bedroom and living room furniture. This was the first time Denise or I ever had new beds. With a few trips to the local department store and some hand-me-downs from Cindy, which I greatly appreciated, we had everything we needed.

With my limited income, we still qualified for government health insurance and food assistance. Just when I thought I had seen the best of my sister and her family's kindness, Cindy and Lindsey showed up at my door with a large storage container. They walked in, one on each side, and removed the lid from the container. There was every kind of hygiene and cleaning product imaginable. I will never forget my sister's kind words that day. She said, "Here are some things we thought you might need that you can't buy with your food card." I thanked Cindy and Lindsey and thought to myself, *I hope someday I can give to others in need as freely and generously as my sister and her family do.*

Things were going well for Denise and me at our new place, but we still didn't attend a church. I could feel the Holy Spirit tugging at me, but I refused to listen. The following year my other daughter, Vickey, came to live with us. I quickly found myself raising two teenage daughters, and at the time I needed the Lord the most, I continued to reject Him.

Shortly after the girls turned sixteen, they got their first jobs and a car. A couple of years later, my daughters graduated and left home. It didn't take long to realize that my children's lives were not going in the direction I had hoped. I had five children, two boys and three girls, and a stepdaughter, whom I dearly loved as my own daughter. All of the girls were pregnant before they were married. My oldest son was separated from his wife, and my youngest son would not speak to me. I thought to myself, *O Lord, my God, what have I done?* I began to realize that I didn't provide them with the Christ-centered foundation that they needed to be successful in life. When I say successful, I do not mean big houses or fancy cars. I simply meant serving the Lord. I believe that most parents have regrets, and I was no different. My biggest regret was that I didn't get my children involved in church at an early age. After much prayer, I received my answer, "Follow Me and lead by example." By the love and grace of God, some of my children did come to know Jesus Christ as their Lord and Savior. I prayed daily for the ones who did not know Jesus.

Living at the little apartment complex was a blessing for me. The people who lived there were more like family than neighbors. Later my mother and my aunt Jane also moved there. We went to one another's apartments for dinner, snacks, and movies. I sometimes wonder how many lives could have been changed if we would have had Bible studies. With Denise and Vickey out on their own, I was starting to experience empty nest syndrome. I was feeling lonely, and instead of turning to the Lord, I turned to the local taverns. I started hanging out and drinking with old friends who seemed to be sitting on the same barstools when I left fifteen years earlier. I didn't feel like I fit in, but that didn't stop me from trying. Almost every weekend I was at a bar, and if I wasn't, I thought I was missing something. What I was really missing was my Lord and Savior, Jesus Christ. *How I have strayed! This can't be the path He laid out for me, but how do I get back?* I asked myself.

CHAPTER 8

But he said to me, "My grace is sufficient for
you, for my power is made perfect in weakness.
Therefore, I will boast all the more gladly
about my weaknesses, so that Christ's power
may rest on me. That is why, for Christ's
sake, I delight in weaknesses, in insults, in
hardships, in persecutions, in difficulties.
For when I am weak, then I am strong.

—2 Corinthians 12:9–10

M Y OLDEST SON, Andy, had just returned home from the
military after serving a number of years, and I was giving
him a long-winded lecture about higher education. I was shocked
and even a little angry when he challenged me and said, "What
about you, Dad? You don't even have a high school diploma!" At
first, I thought, *How dare he speak to me like that!* However, I soon
realized that my son did not mean any disrespect. He was just
trying to make the point that he was not ready for college yet.

I was talking to my friend Jenny about my conversation with
Andy, and she didn't waste any time blurting out, "He's right!
What about you?" I was angry at her, but I knew she was right.
Eighth grade was the highest grade level that I had completed, so
I didn't believe higher education was possible for me. Jenny started

by making subtle comments about what a good adult education program our local state university had. "Why don't you give them a call?" she asked.

"I will!" I replied. I didn't have any intention of calling about adult education, but I underestimated how persistent she could be!

A few days later, Jenny dropped off some children's books so I could practice reading. I wasn't interested in the books, but I was sure if I didn't call the university, my friend wouldn't give me a moment of peace. I eventually called the adult education department. A pleasant man answered the telephone and said, "Hello! ABLE."

I replied, "Hi, Able, my name is Bill Richmond, and I am interested in taking classes for the GED."

The man chuckled and said, "My name is not Able! My name is Dennis. ABLE is the name of the program. It stands for adult basic literacy education."

I felt foolish after using the wrong name, but I pressed forward and told Dennis that I wanted to take classes. I also mentioned I had some problems. I went on to say, "I'm blind."

Dennis replied, "We can make accommodations."

I continued, "But I have one leg, and you're on the second floor."

He calmly replied, "We have an elevator."

In a panic, I blurted out, "I live ten miles away!"

He said, "There is public transportation that comes to the campus every hour." Dennis was nearly as persistent as my friend Jenny was! It wasn't long before I called our local public transportation system, and the following week they picked me up right on time.

My first day was spent taking a placement test. I knew my test scores were going to be low, but I was more embarrassed to find out that I was between a fourth- and fifth-grade reading level. I was certain that I couldn't pass the GED exam, but by the grace of God, I stopped drinking and started studying!

For the next six months, I studied five days a week and eight hours a day. The GED classes were above the college library, and from time to time, I would wander over to the college cafeteria. I would try to eat my lunch when classes were in session, so I didn't have to encounter as many college students. I was sure they thought that I was too old to be in school and not very smart. To my surprise, I passed the exit exam, and Dennis said that I was ready to take the GED test as soon as he could schedule it.

While I was waiting for the test to be scheduled, I mustered up the courage to stop in and talk to an academic advisor. She assured me that if I passed the GED test, I would do just fine in college. I half-heartedly believed the woman, but I wanted to focus on the GED first. During a walk around the campus, I realized that there were more students my age than I thought. I didn't think about college any more until I passed the GED test.

Passing the test was not easy, but I accomplished it. They provided an examiner who read the test aloud to me. I was also granted extra time, and I used every bit of it. I was there for eleven hours! After about six hours into the test, the examiner asked if I was going to stop for lunch. When I declined the offer, she pulled a muffin out of her lunch bag. With a puzzled look on her face, she extended her arm with the muffin in her hand and said, "Please eat this!" I believe she thought that I was going to fall out of the chair from hunger! I accepted her offer and ate the muffin. In five more hours, I completed the test, and now there wasn't anything else to do but wait.

Dennis asked me to be a guest speaker at the graduation ceremony, and I gladly accepted his offer. As I waited patiently to see if I graduated, I received my answer the same day as the ceremony. Finally, the email arrived that I had been waiting for. I held my breath as I leaned over the computer and clicked on the link with my mouse. I sat in front of the monitor in some sort of trancelike state. I couldn't believe that I had passed! After

I snapped out of my trance and realized that it was true, I thought to myself, *By the grace of God, I accomplished something!*

ABLE faculty and staff handed my diploma off from car to car and exit by exit in a relay that was more than two hundred miles long so that I would have my diploma in time for the graduation ceremony! It arrived with thirty minutes to spare. The speaking engagement was a wonderful opportunity to tell the audience what a great teacher Dennis had been and what an awesome experience ABLE was!

Summer was approaching soon, but that was the least of my thoughts. I had a feeling of unrest, almost as if there was something else I needed to do. I was praying earnestly every day. I was sure the Holy Spirit was leading me down a path, but I wasn't sure where. I still didn't have a church, but I was searching. I knew my life was on the brink of changing, but nothing could have prepared me for how much. I couldn't shake the feeling of unrest. With a GED, the possibilities were endless!

A short time later, I went back to the college and took the placement exam. My academic advisor said, "Congratulations! You are a college student!" My vision was gradually getting worse, so a friend of mine recommended speech recognition software. My first two classes were math and English. The software worked well for the English class but not for the math class. I was amazed when I received my grades for the first semester. I earned an A in English and a B+ in math. I was so proud of my accomplishments that tears welled up in my eyes, but I was sure it wasn't anything I did. I felt stronger than ever that the Lord had something special for me to do. By the next two semesters, I was going to school full-time. My vision continued to get worse, but by the grace of God, I still maintained a respectable GPA.

In September of 2008, I was at our local street festival, the same one where my stepmother approached me years before to come and visit my biological father. I was mesmerized when the praise band from a nearby church went by on a float, blasting their music. I was watching the parade with my friend Jenny and her family. Almost simultaneously, Jenny and I turned to each other and said, "I wouldn't mind trying that church!"

Later that day I mentioned the band to my sister, Cindy, who had not been to church since childhood. I was surprised at her reply. She said, "If I was going to go to church, I would try that one. I think that's the pastor who is on our local radio station. I heard he drives a race car." That was all that I needed to hear. I was curious to find out what this race car-driving pastor was all about!

The following Sunday, Jenny, her family, and I made the fifteen-minute journey to the new church. From the minute we walked in the door, we were welcomed with handshakes and hugs. There was even a nice white-haired lady who grabbed me by the wrist and insisted that she pray for me. I was excited to go back the next week. I couldn't have been happier! I finally had a church. I was attending college, and I had stopped drinking and using drugs. My life was improving greatly!

However, my eyes seemed to be getting worse. It was getting more difficult to see the hands on my kitchen clock, and when I went shopping with my friends, it was getting more difficult to give an honest opinion on the clothes they were buying. It was even more and more difficult to shop for myself. I caught myself holding onto the back of a friend's neck to stop from falling down or running into something. Jenny would tolerate me holding onto her neck, but her daughter was a different story. She would shake her head from side to side until I would let go! The last straw was when I grabbed her son's neck! He was only eight years old, and his mother screeched, "Run! He is going to break your neck!" Jenny and I erupted with laughter, but the harsh reality was that I needed a cane to guide me. I fought the idea of a white cane with a red tip used by individuals with visual impairments or blindness for as long as I could. I knew my mother blamed herself for my premature birth and vision problems. I was sure that it would break my mother's heart to see me with the cane, and I couldn't stand it. However, a short time later, I didn't have any choice but to use one. My mother accepted the idea better than I expected.

My mother had been sick for years with chronic obstructive pulmonary disease (COPD). She passed away in May 2009, but not before I had the honor of leading her to the Lord. As my mother lay on her deathbed, laboring to speak, I asked her, "Mom, do you know where you are going when you die?"

She replied, "Heaven, I hope!"

I gently held her hand and asked, "Would you like to know for sure?" She answered with a nod. "Do you believe that Jesus died on the cross to pay for your sins?" I asked. She nodded again. "Do you believe He was raised on the third day?" She nodded again. "Do you believe Jesus is the Son of God?" Again, she nodded. "Do you repent of your sins and turn your life over to Jesus Christ as your Lord and Savior?"

With a whisper she answered, "Yes!"

"You're a Christian now, and you are going to heaven! The Bible is very clear about this," I said as I kissed her hand. "Mom, please believe me when I say I do not blame you for my vision problem. The Lord has used me in ways he may not have been able to if I would have had perfect vision, and for that I am grateful. Get some rest. I'll be back in a little while."

With a frail whisper, she said, "I love you."

"I love you too, Mom," I replied.

I came back a short time later to find my mother sitting up and eating her lunch like nothing was wrong. I nearly fainted! I spent the rest of the day watching the old shows on television that my mother liked so much.

That night before bed, I got on my knees and thanked the Lord for the wonderful day with my mother. I asked that if He wasn't going to heal her, He would take her quickly. The next day my mother went home to be with the Lord. Once again, I found myself on my knees, praising the Lord and thanking Him for ending her suffering. I prayed, "Lord God, I come to You in thanks. Thank You for ending my mother's suffering. Father, I pray for strength when I attend my mother's funeral. You know, Father, I don't do well at funerals. I pray that I can be a strong shoulder for my family members to cry on. It is in Jesus's name that I pray." I broke down between then and the funeral and shed some tears, but when it came time for the funeral, I was at peace and strong for my family. I stood by the casket welcoming each and every guest as they approached the casket for calling hours. I welcomed guests at the funeral, and again at the graveside services and consoled family members who needed it. I am a very emotional person, and I thought I would be a sobbing mess. Instead, though, the Lord answered my prayer.

He blessed me with the peace of mind of knowing that my mother was with Him. I had missed quite a bit of school while I was helping my sister make the necessary preparations for the funeral, and my grades started to decline. But by the grace of God, I passed all of my classes without having to repeat any of them.

I enjoyed the summer off from school, but the next semester wasn't any easier, especially with my vision continuing to decline. I started using the math and writing labs more often, and I had a florescent light that hung in my bedroom from chains over my computer desk. Homework was taking twice as long, sometimes until 2:00 or 3:00 a.m., and I had to get back up at 7:00 a.m. to catch public transportation and start the next day. The bus dropped me off at the campus at 8:30 in the morning and picked me back up at 5:30 in the evening. That made for a long day, especially if I only had a couple of classes. The following semester I took a full class load, but something had to give.

Jenny took me to one of the best ophthalmologists in the business, and my greatest fear was confirmed. After hours of testing, the doctor came back with the verdict. "You know you have retinopathy of prematurity from birth?" he asked.

"Yes," I replied.

"You also have the characteristics of retinitis pigmentosa," he claimed.

"What does that mean for my vision?" I asked.

"Most people with retinitis pigmentosa will eventually lose most or all of their sight," he stated.

I wasn't surprised, considering how fast my vision was declining; however, now I would have to reevaluate my life. I spent a lot of time praying that night. I went through many emotions, including anger. At one point I cried out, "Lord, what do You want me to do? Just reveal it to me!" I woke up in the morning with the same calmness I had felt at my mother's funeral. School wasn't getting easier, but I felt like I was where I should be, at least until the Lord revealed something different.

CHAPTER 9

"For I know the plans I have for you," declares
the Lord, "plans to prosper you and not to harm
you, plans to give you hope and a future."

—Jeremiah 29:11

M Y NEW CHURCH was everything I expected it to be. In fact, I even joined the single adult ministry group. Everyone made me feel welcome. Although it was a single's group, I wasn't looking for anything more than some new friends to hang out with.

A short time later, the group had a game night where we invited other local churches to join us. I mingled with other singles, and we played video games and board games. With my limited vision, it was difficult. However, my new friends were always there to help me out when I needed it. The game night was great fun, and the prettiest lady in the place was checking me out. However, I was clueless.

Another singles event I attended was a bicycle ride at our local national park. I rode a tandem bike with one of the other church members for twenty-five miles. That was the first time I was on a bike in more than twenty years, but we made it back with only a few mishaps. Because of my prosthetic leg, I could only get off the bike on the left side, but the person in the front kept forgetting. We fell three times, and I got my pant leg caught in the chain. But it was a good ride, and we made it back to join our group safe and sound. The same attractive lady from the game night was standing at the pavilion and waiting for our group with a camera pointed at us, but again, I was still clueless.

My next encounter with the mysterious lady was at a Bible study. My friends Jenny, Janet, and I were sitting at a table in the back of the room. Janet was quick to ask, "Why does that woman keep looking back here?"

Jenny replied, "I don't know!"

Janet blurted out, "I think she's looking at Bill!"

Jenny burst out laughing, and I snickered and said, "I doubt it!"

A week later the mystery came to an end. After church I used the men's room as I usually did every week, but this week I heard the voice of an angel when I came out. The cutest voice ever was calling my name! She said, "Will, Will! It's Abbey, Abbey White!" Abbey was standing in the hall straight across from the men's room. She said, "I'm sorry to hear about your mother's passing. My mother passed away last year. If you want someone to talk to, just let me know." I quickly started rattling off my contact information, and she was writing it in her checkbook as fast as I was saying it.

My youngest daughter, Denise, came over just in time to see her finish writing. I introduced her to Abbey, and that seemed to go well. Abbey said, "I'm going camping for five days. I'll call you when I get back."

"Okay!" I replied with a big smile on my face. When my daughter and I were far enough away so Abbey couldn't hear, I asked, "Is she as pretty as I think she is?"

Denise stated, "She is really pretty, Dad!"

"I thought so," I replied.

"I guess you did because you gave her your cell phone number, your home phone number, and your email!" Denise chuckled and then asked, "Are you sure you didn't forget anything?"

"I hope not!" I exclaimed.

Just like she promised, I received a phone call from Abbey when she returned from her camping trip. My head was inches from the computer monitor as I studied for a test when the phone rang. I was so involved in my studies that it startled me! I wondered who could be calling at this time of night. I was pleasantly surprised when I heard her voice coming from the phone. "Hi, is this Will?" she asked. Before I could reply, she said, "It's Abbey from church."

"Hi!" I replied. My head was spinning with all kinds of thoughts. When I joined the single adult ministry group, one of the leaders of the group introduced me as "Will," and I never corrected him. So everyone in the group now called me Will instead of Bill. The new name sounded strange to me; however, I had no intention of correcting her. We began to talk about my mother's passing, but I quickly conveyed to her that I was okay with it all because I was able to lead my mother to Christ before she died. Abbey was glad to hear this. "I still miss my mother from time to time, but there is comfort in knowing that she is with the Lord!" I replied. Before long, we were off the topic of my mother, but it seemed like there was more to say.

I couldn't believe we had been talking for nearly four hours! We talked about our finances, previous marriages, and everything in between. In just four hours, it felt like I had gained a best friend! We said our goodbyes, and I got ready for bed. But when I lay down, it was no surprise that I couldn't sleep. My mind was racing with thoughts. *Did she just call to be nice, or is she interested in me?* I thought to myself. For a brief moment, I even wondered if my mother from heaven sent an angel my way!" If she was interested in me, I was sure it had to be some kind of divine intervention! Thankfully, the following day was Tuesday, and I didn't have any classes, so I could sleep in.

After tossing and turning all night, I woke up, and the first thought that came to my mind was Abbey. Around lunchtime my curiosity got the best of me. I had to find out if she was interested in me, so I just picked up the phone and called. I was somewhat surprised that she answered. I heard the same sweet voice coming from the phone. She said, "Hello, Will."

"Hello!" I replied. "Some friends and I are going to the park around six o'clock to hear a band." I went silent with an uncomfortable pause. Then I just said, "Would you like to join us?"

"Sure! I can meet you there right after work," she replied.

I gave her directions and said, "See you this evening. Goodbye!" She said goodbye, and I hung up the phone and just stared at it. I started replaying the conversation over in my head. *Something is different*, I thought to myself. *She seemed excited to go.* Then it hit me like a bolt of lightning. She had called me by my name when she answered the phone! *She has my number programmed into her phone! This means something!* I wasn't sure what it meant, but I liked it.

I called my friend Jenny, who was going to be picking me up to go to the park, and I told her that Abbey from church was going to meet us there. Jenny was wild with excitement! I'm sure her phone was buzzing, telling all of our friends about Abbey and trying to figure out who she was.

A few minutes after we arrived at the park, Abbey also arrived. It must have looked like a church event. My entire group was there. A moment or two later, the band took the stage. After the first song, I looked at Abbey, shrugged my shoulders, and said, "Next time you can choose the entertainment!"

She gave a cute laugh and said, "They're not so bad."

"You are just being nice! It's a just couple of guys with triangles and a flute." Jenny recommended that we go to a local coffee shop for something to drink, and everyone agreed. No one wasted any time getting out of their chairs. I believe everyone was in a hurry to leave. The little band was not appealing to any of us. I had a choice to make. Should I play it safe and ride with Jenny, or should I assume that it's a date and ride with Abbey? Thankfully, I didn't have to make that choice. She didn't know where the coffee shop was, so she asked me to ride with her to show her the way. I gladly accepted her request.

"When you pull out of the parking lot, take a right turn," I said. She did just as I instructed, so I thought this would be a good time to have a little fun. Before we reached the corner, I looked over and said, "Where do we go from here? I'm blind!"

"You really don't know?" she said and gasped.

I let her sweat for just a minute, and then I busted out laughing and said, "Take a left at the corner!" I guided us right to the coffee shop, but when we got inside, the joke was on me.

We went up to the counter to order our drinks, and I started to panic. *Should I offer to pay? Will she think I am being too pushy?* I wondered. I had a bad experience with a woman at a department store the week before. When I held the door open for her, she gave me a dirty look and said, "Don't you think I can open my own door?" I didn't want to mess it up with Abbey. While I was planning my strategy, Abbey was getting her wallet out of her purse, and Jenny looked back and said, "You don't have to pay, Abbey. I'll get yours." There I stood between the two women. I felt like the biggest cheapskate in the world! My friend threw me right under the bus. All I could do was grab my wallet as fast as I could and say, "I got it!" By this time, it was me that was sweating. I barely pulled that one off!

We all had our drinks and went to the patio where we found a large table that would accommodate all of us. Abbey moved her chair close to mine, and even with my declining sight, I could see the big smile on her face! We had a great time at the coffee shop, but I was still asking myself if Abbey was attracted to me or if she was sitting close to me just to give the person on the other side of her more room. I knew what I needed, and that was a woman's perspective.

I rode home with Jenny, and we decided to visit her daughter, Janet. I asked Jenny to give me her opinion about the evening. It was like poking a stick into a bee's nest. She said, "I think she likes you, but you're going to mess it up by being so cheap!"

"I was just nervous. Remember how the woman acted at the store when I held the door open for her?" I rebuked.

"Well, who is it?" Janet wanted to know. "Is it the lady from the Bible study?"

"Yes, that's her. She seems very nice," Jenny said.

Janet exclaimed, "I told you so! I told you she was looking at Bill!"

"I think his new name is Will. At least that's what Abbey calls him!" Jenny joked.

"Will? That's not his name!" Janet yelled.

"Does anyone mind if I join the conversation?" I asked. By this time, they were having too much fun to give me the floor, but I pushed my way into the conversation and said, "I just haven't corrected her on my name yet. Besides, everyone in the single's group calls me Will."

They weren't done having fun yet. They chanted simultaneously, "Will, Will, Will!" Jenny and Janet are dear friends. They were just having a little fun at my expense, and I really didn't mind.

After the fun was over, Jenny said, "I think she really does like you!"

"Do you think so?" I asked.

"Yes, I think she does," she replied.

"That's what I was hoping you would say, but I have never dated a Christian girl before," I replied. By the time the night was over, we concluded that Abbey was attracted to me.

The following day I invited Abbey to go out for coffee and dessert at a local restaurant. We both ordered the rice pudding, but just as the pudding was being served, Abbey's cell phone rang. She answered her phone, but I could tell she was in a hurry to end the conversation. "That was my daughter Angeline. She was sitting across the street, watching us," she said. Abbey was a little embarrassed.

"You can't be too careful these days," I said. "Why don't you call her back and ask her to join us?"

"She's on her way home now. I think she just wanted to see who the mysterious man was!" she said and chuckled.

My mind raced with thoughts. *She told her daughter about me, and her daughter came to check me out. This can only mean one thing! She's attracted to me.* I didn't want to get too lost in thought, so I smiled at her and said, "Don't be embarrassed about your daughter sitting across the street. I think that says a lot about the both of you."

"It does?" Abbey asked.

"Yes, it does. It says that you and your daughter are very close. Also, she is protective of you, and you are very honest." I said.

"Yes, we are very close, and she is a little overprotective. But where did the honesty come from?"

"You didn't have to tell me who was on the phone, and I wouldn't have asked," I replied.

Abbey and I saw each other almost every day for the next two weeks. We held hands and walked on the beach. We talked about our pasts, our hopes, and our dreams, and it was as if our lives were open books. Things couldn't have been going better. It seemed like we could tell each other anything. Something was happening very fast that scared both of us. Not long after that, I got the dreaded "Dear John" email. Abbey wrote, "Things are moving too fast, and we should stop seeing each other." I stared at the computer in disbelief, asking myself, "What do I do now?" Abbey and I had fallen for each other very fast, and I was sure what we had for the past two weeks was very real; however, I knew that I had to respect her wishes. I told myself, "If it is meant to be, it will be. If not, it never was." I felt like I at least owed Abbey a response. I thought to myself, *This may be the last time she hears from me. I'd better make it count!* I returned the email, wished her well, and thanked her for the good times I had with her over the past few weeks.

School was out for the summer, so I spent the next five days praying and listening to four Christian audiobooks about relationships. The Lord blessed me with peace about the situation. I wasn't sure what the future had to bring, but I was confident that it was going to be all right. The following week I received an email from Abbey. She wanted to know how I was doing. I responded by saying, "As well as can be expected, but I listened to four books about relationships because I didn't want to mess up the next one." She told me she was impressed that I would read books to learn about relationships, and we both agreed that we wanted to try again, but much slower this time. She later told me that although she had been scared, she missed me terribly.

CHAPTER 10

A wife of noble character who can find? She is
worth far more than rubies. Her husband has full
confidence in her and lacks nothing of value. She
brings him good, not harm, all the days of her life.

—Proverbs 31:10–12

I DON'T BELIEVE Abbey or I knew the meaning of slow because
we were engaged four months later. We had a whirlwind
relationship, and we saw each other almost every day. My past
relationships ended in disaster. I began to pray that God would
bless this marriage. I put the books I read on healthy relationships
into practice. I was determined to treat my fiancé like a princess.

My sight was beginning to decline rapidly, but I insisted on
opening Abbey's car door. One day she picked me up for church,
and like usual, I opened the car door for her; however, this time
she wasn't getting in. I must have given her an odd look as if to
say, "Why aren't you getting in?" She covered her mouth and
said, "I can't drive from the back seat!"

I burst out laughing, realizing that I had opened the back door
instead and said, "I guess you can't!" It wasn't the first mishap,
and I was sure it wouldn't be my last.

It was time to start looking for wedding rings, and it was
important to me that Abbey had a nice set of rings. One day,

while shopping at the mall with a friend, some rings caught my eye. I was sure they were way beyond my budget. I asked the clerk to see them. Even with my declining sight, I could see that they were every bit as beautiful as I thought. I remarked how much I thought my fiancé would love the rings, but they were out of my budget. The saleslady leaned in close to tell me, "I have a 20 percent off coupon, and in two weeks we are going to be having a sale with an additional 20 to 60 percent savings on wedding sets." I gave the sales lady a small deposit to hold the rings until I could bring Abbey in to see them.

A few days later, armed with my coupon and ready to bargain, we arrived at the store. I was determined to get the rings for my beautiful fiancé. Abbey loved the rings every bit as much as I knew she would. "They're beautiful, but they look like they're too expensive!" she exclaimed. I laid the coupon on the counter, and the clerk grabbed her calculator. With all of the discounts, I was still nearly one hundred dollars over budget. My heart sank!

Abbey began looking through the glass display case. I was sure she was going to pick something that she really didn't want just to stay within the budget. I was ready to spend the extra hundred dollars until the clerk said, "Hold on a minute. Let me try something." She returned with a wedding band identical to the one I had picked out but with just slightly smaller diamonds. I was able to purchase the beautiful set of rings, and I didn't break my budget!

The sales clerk measured Abbey's finger and offered to send the rings in immediately to get them sized. She wanted to get the rings sized as fast as possible, but I made an excuse to take them with us and bring them back later. I had plans for the rings that very day in October of 2009. I didn't want to wait one more day to officially propose! On the way home I asked, "Why don't we take a ride by the lake?" We went to the lake to sit on the bench where we frequently watched the sunset. The cold wind was blowing across the lake, and the waves were crashing against the shore with a loud roar! I pulled the ring out of my pocket and got on one knee in front of the bench. Almost before I could ask, "Will you marry me?" she was in tears, shaking her head and muttering the words, "Yes! Yes! Yes!" The roar of the waves was so loud that she later told me that she didn't hear a word I said but that she knew I was proposing the minute I dropped to one knee!

Now that we were engaged, it was time to start planning the wedding. Abbey's three wishes were a beautiful wedding dress, great food, and a fun night of dancing. I wanted a limo and a wonderful day with family and friends. We were on a budget, but I was determined to give my soon-to-be bride the wedding she always wanted! She took care of picking out her wedding dress and the dresses for the maid of honor and the bridesmaids. I picked out the tuxedos for the men and me. We were going to be married at our church.

The big day was finally here! When I arrived at the church, I was met at the door by Abbey's daughter and maid of honor, Angeline. She was taking care of every detail and making sure everything went as planned. I was dressed with twenty minutes to spare, but we couldn't find my tie. Everyone searched franticly, but the tie wasn't to be found. I met Angeline at the top of the stairs. "Only a few minutes to go. Are you about ready?" she asked.

"All but my tie. They didn't put it in with my tux!" I exclaimed. The big smile on her face quickly disappeared! With fifteen minutes left until the wedding ceremony began, we had to come up with a solution for the missing tie!

My brother-in-law drove me to the local department store. I quickly picked out a tie to match my tux, and we made it back to the church with a few minutes to spare. The next thing I remember is that the men and I were on the stage with the preacher, waiting for my bride to come down the aisle. It was all I could do to hold back the tears, and it didn't help matters that my sisters were in the first few rows, crying at full speed. The pianist began to play as the most beautiful bride in the world walked down the aisle, soon to become my wife!

Once the ceremony was finished, and the pictures were taken, the limo drove us to the reception. It was held at a local banquet hall, and it was everything we had hoped it would be! We had invited 125 of our closest family and friends. The food was outstanding. The cake was fabulous, and our guests danced the night away! We had an incredible night, but more than that, I received a beautiful bride—the privilege of marrying my best friend and the godly woman I had always hoped for.

We planned a wonderful week for our honeymoon in a magnificent city near where Abbey lived as a child. We had an incredible time taking in the sights, taking a ride on a riverboat cruise down a beautiful scenic river, and enjoying a fabulous chicken and rib dinner. We ate at an exquisite restaurant on the top of a mountain with an amazing view of where rivers meet with a fountain joining them. If the honeymoon was any indication of what was to come, then I couldn't wait to get back to home to begin our new life together as husband and wife!

Once we arrived home, our schedules were back to normal. Abbey was working full-time, and I was one semester away from an associate degree. We loved our small town. We lived in a nice subdivision with a big backyard. One of our wedding gifts was a huge smoker that fit perfectly on our back patio. By the end of the summer, we had smoked everything! We smoked ribs, brisket, and I could smoke a half-dozen whole chickens at one time!

I received an associate degree in the fall, and Abbey made a career change that would require some additional schooling. I continued going to school working toward a bachelor's degree, and she finished the classes that she needed. We had a choice to make before the next semester. Abbey had to finish her internship at one of the major hospital systems in the city, which required a lot of driving in the winter. With the unpredictable winters in our area, and since I could finish my schooling online, we chose to move to a high-rise closer to the city. Abbey finished her internship and graduated and then went to work in one of the other major hospitals in the area.

I finished the required classes to complete a bachelor's degree; however, I still needed to complete an internship. After thinking long and hard where I would intern, our local transportation system was my final choice. Abbey asked, "What are you going to be doing there?"

"I'm not sure, but I'm interested in finding out how local government works," I replied. I wrote and gave speeches to different groups. I worked with the outreach department on community projects, and I worked in public relations on some rebranding issues. It was a great experience, and I gained some lifelong friends in the process.

My time there was over, and my schooling was finished. I graduated with a bachelor's degree in communications with academic honors. I was inducted into an honor society for communication majors, and I received the senior scholar award.

The time finally came for my graduation ceremony. My class came into the auditorium in a single-file line to the beat of our school song, and we took our seats. I waited with anticipation for my name to be called. As much as I tried, I still wasn't prepared to hear the dean say, "William Richmond ... with honors!" Tears welled up in my eyes as I tapped my way to the podium with my white cane to receive my diploma with two honor cords around my neck. My family, my friends, and my wife were there as I tried to imagine the looks on their faces, holding back tears of joy! I accepted my diploma and returned to my seat, thinking to myself, *This is a God moment!* My head raced with thoughts. *I started this educational venture with an eighth-grade education and a fifth-grade reading level. I had never solved an algebra problem, and I had never read a novel cover to cover until I attended college!* I wanted to ask myself how this could happen, but I already knew the answer. The Lord was preparing me to serve Him. I wasn't sure how I would use my education to serve the Lord, but I was sure there was nothing I would rather do.

CHAPTER 11

The righteous cry out, and the Lord hears them; he
delivers them from all their troubles. The Lord is
close to the brokenhearted and saves those who are
crushed in spirit. The Lord redeems his servants; no
one will be condemned who takes refuge in him.

—Psalm 34:17–18, 22

THANK YOU, GOD, for allowing me to go through what I
had to go through, so that I could become who I am. I
have heard it said, "It doesn't matter where a person starts. What
matters is where they finish." You have proven this to be true
in my life over and over again. From birth, when my body was
lifeless and blue, You spared my life. During my childhood when
I faced abuse and neglect, You gave me the strength to overcome
it. I made bad choices during my teenage years that could have
destroyed my life. I began to use drugs and dropped out of school
in the ninth grade, but again, You were there. I had children out
of wedlock and two failed marriages, but You still loved me. After
being struck by a hit-and-run driver while I was walking down
that dark lonely road and left for dead, You carried me to safety.
All of this before I even knew You.

Thank You, Father, for putting Ryan, my friend, my mentor,
and the person who led me to you, in my life. Through a random

act of kindness, Ryan was able to lead me to You, and my life has been transformed in ways that are beyond my wildest imagination. You gave me the privilege of leading my mother to You while she was on her deathbed. You gave me the strength, courage, and wisdom to go back to school and eventually to college and graduate with honors.

Just when I thought life couldn't get any better, You introduced me to the many women I so dearly love. I love the godly Christian woman. I love the honorable one. I love the incredibly smart woman. I love the sensitive one. I love the woman who always puts her family first. I love the strong-willed woman who stands up for what she believes in. I love the woman who covers her mouth, whose face gets red so easy, and I love the woman who is my best friend. Thank You, Father, for blessing me with these women. They are all one beautiful woman, my wife, Abbey Richmond.

After starting so weak, thank You for letting me finish so strong. Father, it is my hope and my prayer that every person who reads this book will finish strong. I'm certain if You can use a wretch like me, there is hope for all. I spent so many years searching for love, happiness, hope, and purpose. If I would have only known You were just waiting for me, I could have avoided what seemed like a lifetime of misery. I'm not looking back with regret. As I have said before, "I'm happy to have gone through what I did to become who I am." This book is just a small contribution to what You have given me. Father, thank You for sending Your only Son, Jesus Christ, to die on the cross to pay for my sins because You love me so much. Thank You, Father for the love, happiness, hope, and joy that only you can provide.

MY PRAYER FOR
THE READER

I pray that you know that Jesus Christ is the Son of God. I pray that you will ask Him into your life right now to be your Lord and Savior. I pray that you will repent of your sins. I pray that you know that He died on the cross to pay for your sins. I pray that you know that God raised his Son, Jesus Christ, to sit at his side as your Lord and Savior. It is only through the blood of Christ that your sins can be forgiven. If you haven't already taken this step of faith, I pray that you will. I pray that you will tell someone else how Christ has transformed your life so they might ask Him into their life as well. That way, we can all experience God's kingdom together.

Lord God, I pray that you can use this book in a mighty way, but if only one person comes to know You, that's okay as well. I am honored that you chose me to write this book.